ASK

FAITH QUESTIONS IN A SKEPTICAL AGE

Ask
Faith Questions in a Skeptical Age

Book
978-1-5018-0333-8
978-1-5018-0334-5 eBook

DVD
978-1-5018-0337-6

Leader Guide
978-1-5018-0335-2
978-1-5018-0336-9 eBook

For more information, visit AbingdonPress.com.

Also by Scott J. Jones

The Wesleyan Way: A Faith That Matters

*The Future of The United Methodist Church:
Seven Vision Pathways (Ed. with Bruce Ough)*

Staying at the Table: The Gift of Unity for United Methodists

*The Evangelistic Love of God and Neighbor:
A Theology of Witness and Discipleship*

United Methodist Doctrine: The Extreme Center

John Wesley's Conception and Use of Scripture

Scott J. Jones and Arthur D. Jones

ASK

Faith Questions in a Skeptical Age

Abingdon Press / Nashville

ASK:
FAITH QUESTIONS IN A SKEPTICAL AGE

ISBN 978-1-5018-0333-8

15 16 17 18 19 20 21 22 23 24—10 9 8 7 6 5 4 3 2 1
MANUFACTURED IN THE UNITED STATES OF AMERICA

Contents

Introduction. 7

1. Can Only One Religion Be True? 11

2. Why Is There Suffering and Evil? 27

3. How Can I Believe in Science and Creation? 41

4. How Can I Believe in a God I Can't Prove?. 55

5. Can I Trust the Old Testament? 71

6. Are Marriage, Sex, and Family Life Religious Issues? 85

7. Was Jesus' Resurrection Real? 99

8. Why Do Christians Disagree About So Many Things? 113

Notes. 126

Introduction

"Ask, and you will receive." (Matthew 7:7)

Go ahead—ask your question. Jesus will not mind. We promise. In fact, when Jesus was teaching and preaching, he made sure he was available to be questioned. He was questioned by everyone from religious leaders to his closest friends. They had finally found someone who could provide answers to the questions of their faith and world.

When you read the stories about Jesus, though, you'll see that he rarely provided answers that were as clear as people wanted. Jesus did not come to earth as a kind of religious precursor to Google. So, ask your questions, but know that Jesus wants us to have more than the right answers. Jesus wants us to go beyond simple data or knowledge to gain wisdom.

Jesus once asked his disciples a simple question: "Who do you say that I am?" Peter responded with a quick answer: "You are the Christ, the Son of the living God" (Matthew 16:15). This, of course, was accurate. Peter's knowledge, though, wasn't enough to keep him from missing the point and having Jesus refer to Satan just a few verses later (16:22-23). Early in his ministry, Peter lacked wisdom to understand the question asked, even if he knew the right answer.

It is easy today to think that Christianity is all about getting the right answer. After all, Christianity in many ways is founded upon the historical claim of the first Easter. Christians believe that Jesus rose from the grave. All of Christianity hangs upon this one piece of information, or, as Paul says in 1 Corinthians 15:17, "If Christ hasn't been raised, then your faith is worthless." Reliance on this one assertion makes Christianity unique. In his book *Atheist Delusions*, David Bentley Hart writes that "Christianity is the only major faith built entirely around a single historical claim."[1] Its importance is evident when we read how Peter began his public ministry. Peter and his disciples stood up to preach one primary claim: "This Jesus, God raised up. We are all witnesses to that fact" (Acts 2:32).

However, Christianity is more than information. It is a revelation and a connecting point between normal human experience and the ultimate reality of the universe. Humanity came to know more clearly than ever before who God is, who we are, and what it means to live well. This is more than information or even knowledge; it is wisdom. We, like Peter, need wisdom. Consider this prayer of Paul in Ephesians 1:17-19.

> I pray that the God of our Lord Jesus Christ, the Father of glory, will give you a spirit of wisdom and revelation that makes God known to you. I pray that the eyes of your heart will have enough light to see what is the hope of God's call, what is the richness of God's glorious inheritance among believers, and what is the overwhelming greatness of God's power that is working among us believers. This power is conferred by the energy of God's powerful strength.

Paul's prayer for the church in Ephesus is not about an intellectual grasp of information, but about a redeemed life marked by the wisdom of God.

Our world, though, is increasingly skeptical that there is any wisdom in following God, or even in believing that God exists. We ask many questions that were never answered in Sunday school. Legitimate questions about other religions, science, Scripture, community, worship, and the purpose of church stop us from believing that the story of Scripture is true. It isn't as though information about such questions is unavailable; we have more data available than ever before, with the power of Google at our fingertips. In seconds we can pull up tweets from the latest conflict around the world, download more podcasts than we can possibly listen to, and search up something about faith on Wikipedia. A few clicks can lead us to more information about Christianity and other religions than we could ever comprehend. As Christians in the twenty-first century, we must grapple with the fact that everyone in the world has access to data. But data is not wisdom, and data alone does not lead to a good life.

The difference between data and wisdom is clearly shown in the life of a man we know. He got a master's degree in accounting, passed the exam to be a certified public accountant, had four years of work experience in his profession, and moved up in his company so he was managing other accountants. He had all the data anyone could ever want about how to manage money, cash flows, and budgets. Nevertheless, he was broke, living paycheck to paycheck. He bought a new Porsche and lived in an upscale apartment, but he could not pay his bills despite having a significant salary. He had all the data he would ever need but had no wisdom about financial matters. In contrast, a wise person might not know the rules of accounting and might not know how to put together a spreadsheet, but would live within his or her means and seldom have problems paying bills. How much better would it be for a person to combine data and wisdom! That person would be able to budget and live by the budget and also be able to help others lead lives of wisdom as well.

For faith to thrive in the twenty-first century, we must first ask our own questions and then begin to answer the questions of a skeptical world. The amount of data available has increased greatly, but somehow it's become more difficult to find wise answers and live into the hard questions about God, salvation, and faith. The very existence of all that information sometimes obscures Christianity's wise, faithful answers.

In this book we will pose some of the hard questions people ask, then suggest some answers and responses. In doing so, our hope is to move the conversation from knowing data to living with wisdom. Here are the questions:

1. Can only one religion be true?
2. Why is there suffering and evil?
3. How can I believe in science and creation?
4. How can I believe in a God I can't prove?
5. Can I trust the Old Testament?
6. Are marriage, sex, and family life religious issues?
7. Was Jesus' resurrection real?
8. Why do Christians disagree about so many things?

Sometimes we ask these questions for ourselves. But every Christian should also be ready to give a response to others. We have found that when nominally religious people seek answers to faith questions, they often talk to the closest Christian they trust. In one young adult group, a pastor asked, "Where do you go when you need advice or wisdom about faith?" A young woman, who was a self-proclaimed agnostic, pointed to the friend who had brought her to the group and replied, "I ask her."

Every Christian should be prepared not merely to answer the questions that others may pose, but to help move them from seeking answers to seeking wisdom. Christianity has great answers to the hard questions of faith, not just in the fact of Jesus' resurrection but in the transformation that it offers you and me—in this life and the next.

"It is because of God that you are in Christ Jesus. He became wisdom from God for us. This means that he made us righteous and holy, and he delivered us. This is consistent with what was written: The one who brags should brag in the Lord" (1 Corinthians 1:30-31).

1.
Can Only One Religion Be True?

1.
Can Only One Religion Be True?

What's a religion? How many religions are there?

Scholars who study religions have debates about what constitutes a religion and how they ought to be grouped and counted. Here are some estimates of the ten largest religions in the world and the number of followers each has:

- Christianity 2.1 billion
- Islam 1.5 billion
- Hinduism 900 million
- Chinese traditional religion 394 million
- Buddhism 376 million
- Primal/Indigenous 300 million
- African traditional and diasporic religion 100 million
- Sikh 23 million
- Spiritism 15 million
- Judaism 14 million[1]

Most of these religions are actually divided into many different organizations and groups. In the United States, there are more than one hundred different Christian denominations. These are often grouped into families such as Catholic, Protestant, Orthodox, and others. Add to that the number of nondenominational and independent congregations, and the number of Christian groups would be much higher. The same is true of other religions.

There are many varieties of Islam, not all of which recognize each other as genuine Muslims. Muslims are often grouped into families such as Sunni, Shia, and Sufi. Buddhism has many different sects and schools, and even Judaism is organized into at least three main branches.

Not only are there many different religions, but we are more aware of them than ever. In many places in America, before travel was easy and television was invented, the religious options available to people were limited to the few forms of Christianity present in their town and perhaps a Jewish synagogue. But after 1950, the pattern of religious practice in the United States became more complex. People learned about other religious possibilities, and practitioners of other religions moved into our communities.

The story of Sam, an acquaintance of Scott, gives a perspective on this new way of thinking about religion. When Scott met him, Sam was practicing Sufism. That is a mystical form of Islam in which one dances in a group, chanting praise to God and using the name Allah. Sam participated in Sufi discussion groups, read Sufi literature, and traveled to hear Sufi masters explain their way of worshiping God and living their faith. Sam had been raised as a United Methodist in a town where his mother taught Sunday school and his father was a public school principal. Once Sam got to college, however, he began to practice the Hare Krishna faith, which is based in Hinduism. Then came his conversion to Sufism. Later, he returned to Christianity, but it was a form of Pentecostal Christianity that involved speaking in tongues and miraculous healing of diseases. Being a United Methodist was no longer anywhere on Sam's horizon of personal faith or practice.

Sam's story is an example of the multiple religious options available to spiritual seekers today. Some of these religions teach that there are many different ways of truth, but many of these faiths claim to have an exclusive understanding of truth. In other words, they believe their religion is right and all others are wrong. How should we think about the many different religions? Could all of them be right? Is there only one true religion? In our complex, multicultural, postmodern world, these are important and necessary questions.

The Functions of Religion

Religions have taken a variety of forms throughout human history. Religions are cultural systems that provide answers and practices relating human beings to a perception of ultimate reality. Almost every human culture we know has had at least one religion.

Religions serve a wide variety of functions. They provide answers to the questions about the ultimate reality of the universe. Are there gods? Is there only one God? Where did the universe come from? What is the purpose of the universe? What is my purpose as an individual? Why are things the way they are? What happens after we die? What is moral? What is immoral? How should we live?

In answering such questions, groups of people find common approaches to the many different parts of life. Together they build a common culture and way of life that define many of the values, rituals, beliefs, and moral standards that shape humanity. Religion has shaped many other aspects including ethics, law, government, education, war, peace, economics, and relations among groups of people.

These religions give an account of ultimate reality. Sometimes they have proposed that there are many gods and goddesses. For example, we can learn about the views of the ancient Greeks and Romans from the stories that describe their gods. For the Greeks, Zeus was the king of the gods, Hera was his wife, and Athena, Poseidon, Aphrodite, Ares, Hermes, Hades, Dionysus, and Demeter were among the divine beings whose interactions affected events on earth. The Romans adopted many of the Greek gods for their worship, renaming them Jupiter, Juno, Minerva, Neptune, Venus, Mars, Mercury, Pluto, Bacchus, and Ceres. Greek and Roman temples can be found throughout the former Roman Empire, and the residue of their mythology can be found in our art, our literature, and many names used in Western culture. During the first century A.D., Christians started coming to terms with how they would relate to other religions. The origin of Christianity as a renewal movement within Judaism and their subsequent separation started a long and complex relationship between the two religions. The centuries-long conflict between Christianity and Islam made this question even more difficult.

The situation became more complex as the world became smaller and human knowledge of various cultures increased. Scholars in the field of religious studies now understand more than ever before about the wide variety of religions practiced throughout human history. Such knowledge helps followers of one religion understand the beliefs and practices of others, but it also helps each religion understand its own origins and sacred texts.

For example, biblical scholars help people see that the Bible is best understood when seen in light of the surrounding cultures of the time in which it was written. The story of Abraham's preparation to sacrifice Isaac seems completely wrong to modern minds. How could God so mislead Abraham to believe that he should kill his precious and long-awaited child? But Abraham's situation becomes more understandable when one learns that surrounding cultures of that time worshiped a god called Molech, whose religion required the killing of one's firstborn son. In other words, God was teaching Abraham a lesson that he was not like Molech. In the New Testament, it seems odd to modern readers that Paul gives advice about food for sale in the marketplace after it had been sacrificed to the god of another religion (1 Corinthians 8). But when one thinks of the commandment to worship the one true God and avoid idolatry, we realize that Paul is wrestling with a genuine dilemma faced by first-century Christians.

Our modern situation raises many significant questions for people professing or considering Christianity. Sam's journey from one religion to the next was shaped by a variety of experiences in a university community. He encountered good people who professed Hare Krishna and Sufi beliefs and practiced them, so he tried them out. He was educated in the disciplines of modern science, and many of his professors at the university were atheists who thought any belief in God to be irrational and primitive. He might have taken courses in cultural anthropology and studied many different religions. The world he encountered turned out to be much more complex than he had been taught as a child in Sunday school.

Beyond Sam's university education, the emergence of instantaneous worldwide news coverage showed him the problems of religious violence between Christian groups in Northern Ireland, between Muslims and Christians in Nigeria, between communist authorities and Christians living in certain countries. Yet he yearned to experience a genuine connection with God, so he kept trying out new religions to see if one would fit. Sam's journey is not unique. Many others have followed similar paths, ending up with a wide variety of outcomes.

The Question

Given all this data, what constitutes true wisdom about religion? Can only one religion be true? Let's examine four possible approaches to the question—relativism, agnosticism, atheism, and religion—along with positives and negatives for each one.

Relativism

Relativism is a position that says there are no absolute truths that are universally applicable. Instead, truth is relative to each individual's perspective or context. People often espouse this view in saying, "That may be true for you, but it is not true for me." Relativists might say that each culture has its own religion, and all are equally valuable. This has great appeal in our modern, individualistic society, because all of us can have our own religion and make up whatever beliefs appeal to us. In addition, relativism places a premium on individual choice, tolerance, and mutual respect. It allows for picking and choosing the best things from each religion and combining them to form one's own unique approach to life.

The downside of relativism is it gives up on truth and is internally incoherent. To say both "There is one God" and "There are many gods" is self-contradictory. Or to say that "Jesus is God" and "Krishna is God" is to invoke very different understandings of who God is and what God means for human life here and now. Relativism means that truth is not an objective entity that can be described.

Agnosticism

When people think carefully about relativism, it is easy for them to move into another possibility, agnosticism. The word has ancient Greek roots, in which *a* means "not" and *gnostic* means "knowing." Agnosticism means not knowing what is true. Someone can coherently affirm that there may be a truth about God but that human beings have no way of knowing what it is. When asked, "What is the true religion?" agnostics might say, "No one knows." That is more than saying "I don't know." It is an affirmation that even though it may be impossible for anyone to know the right answer, a right answer could in fact exist. Agnostics have the advantage of avoiding a difficult question because the evidence is so hard to evaluate.

The downside of agnosticism is that it tells religious people that their claims to truth are not verifiable, and so they are not holding an intelligent, reasoned opinion. It also devalues religion by saying it is not important for us to choose among faith options, because we cannot be completely certain that one option is right. A third downside to agnosticism is that it restrains people from moving forward with any particular truth or direction. As Yann Martel wrote in his best-selling novel *The Life of Pi*, "To choose doubt as a philosophy in life is akin to choosing immobility as a means of transportation."[2]

Atheism

Another approach is atheism. A popular form of atheism is based on a philosophy called materialism. This is the claim that the material world, composed of matter and energy, constitutes the only reality. This view is appealing, because science tells us that life itself is based on various combinations of matter and energy that have formed randomly over the more than thirteen billion years since the "big bang" origin of the universe. Scientific progress, especially since the publication of Charles Darwin's book *The Origin of Species*, has provided very plausible explanations for most aspects of reality. Materialistic atheists claim that the idea of a god or supernatural being is not necessary to explain anything. The only reality is one that can be measured as matter or energy.

The downside of atheism and its companion philosophy materialism is that they lead to a meaningless and amoral understanding of the world. In a world defined by materialism, the only purpose seems to be survival of one's self or one's species. It can lead to the slogan we've seen on a T-shirt : "Life is a game, and the one who dies with the most toys wins."

Religion

If we reject relativism, agnosticism, and atheism, how do we decide which religion is true? All the religions make claims about ultimate reality, and those claims have implications for how human beings should live their lives. If there is a god, what should our attitude be toward that god? Are there many gods or just one? If God or gods exist, how should we live? Is there a purpose for the world as a whole or for my life as an individual? What happens after I die?

What Religions Have in Common

The adherents of most of the world's major religions would respond to these questions by saying there is a true religion and that one can know the truth and live by it. How does one choose among these religions?

One starting point is to look at what they have in common.

Most religions believe there is a divine being, and most religious people say there is just one God. Most believe there is a spiritual part of each person, often called a soul, which survives after the body dies. Thus, they believe in life after death. Most religions believe that our attitude toward God should involve some form of worship—praise for God and learning God's will through sacred writings or revelation, prayers, and offerings. Most religions teach some sort of moral code about having compassion for all human beings. Most of them teach that behaviors such as lying, stealing, and murder are to be avoided. Most religions are universal, teaching that all human beings are included in God's care and that each person has the opportunity to worship God.

There are exceptions to all the above statements. Some religions are polytheistic—they believe in more than one god. Some religions are tribal and favor one group of people over others. Some religions sanction practices such as killing nonbelievers or abusing the marginalized. Not all religions teach the same beliefs and practices.

To make things more complicated, for each of the major religions listed above, there have been times when followers of that faith have taught and practiced things that violate the core teachings of their religion.

In choosing among religions, it's important to keep in mind that choosing a religion is an act of faith. Religions seek to connect human beings with what they understand to be ultimate reality, and that reality is most often outside the realm of ordinary knowledge. Faith is thus a decision to live our lives according to a set of beliefs—about God, the world, and our purpose in life—that cannot be proven objectively.

It is also true, by the way, that choosing no religion is an act of faith. People who believe in limiting their view of reality to the material world and people who focus on pleasure as the ultimate good are also choosing a way of life. Many people simply go through life without thinking and ultimately find a way of life without making a conscious choice. That, too, is an act of faith.

A Christian Answer

Christians believe it is reasonable to believe in God, and Christian philosophers have sought good explanations for why it makes sense. But ultimately it takes a leap of faith to trust that God is real and that God has been revealed through Jesus of Nazareth as attested in the Bible. People come to this faith in a variety of ways.

Television personality Kirsten Powers wrote an article in *Christianity Today* about her conversion.

> Just seven years ago, if someone had told me that I'd be writing for *Christianity Today* magazine about how I came to believe in God, I would have laughed out loud. If there was one thing in which I was completely secure, it was that I would never adhere to any religion—especially to evangelical Christianity, which I held in particular contempt.[3]

A man whom Powers was dating asked her, "Do you think you could ever believe?" and "Do you think you could keep an open mind about it?" Since she regarded herself as an open-minded person, she agreed to attend a worship service and was invited to join a Bible study. She writes,

> I remember walking into the Bible study. I had a knot in my stomach. In my mind, only weirdoes and zealots went to Bible studies. I don't remember what was said that day. All I know is that when I left, everything had changed. I'll never forget standing outside that apartment on the Upper East Side and saying to myself, "It's true. It's completely true." The world looked entirely different, like a veil had been lifted off it. I had not an iota of doubt. I was filled with indescribable joy.[4]

Scott has his own story about coming to faith. He was raised in a Christian home and had a powerful experience of seeing the church engage the world on issues of social justice, but he was not a believer.

> I was working full-time for The United Methodist Church and its national youth council, but I was not attending church and did not have faith in Christ. One day I was hitchhiking in northeastern Tennessee, and a truck driver stopped to pick up my friend and me. For the next two hours he talked with us about his faith in Christ. I don't remember his name or much of his story. I do remember he was active in a Seventh-day Adventist church. What I remember most strongly is climbing down from the cab of his truck and thinking to myself, "I want the kind of faith that man has." I believe that experience was God's grace working on me. That conversation started a four-year journey in which I sought a relationship with Christ. During that journey, there were other times when God's grace touched me. There were dead ends where I didn't find what I was seeking. There were times when grace came through a book given to me by a friend. God was continually seeking me out and offering me a relationship with him.[5]

Arthur's story is different. He went through confirmation at the age of twelve and was fully aware of his commitment to Christ. He was active in church, youth group, and campus ministry before starting seminary. He describes his spiritual journey this way:

My faith story is one of gradual growth. I grew up in the church and was baptized as a baby. I sang hymns, loved the people in church, and would always tell you that I believed in God. I never had a single day when I claimed to have no faith. Some days I doubted in God, but overall my faith grew. I finally owned my faith at a weekend event as a freshman in high school, where I felt God's presence and knew that God loved me. My life hasn't had one great moment of faith transformation, but countless moments that confirm what I was told as a child—that God loves me.

If the first step is the necessity of making some sort of faith commitment, the second step is recognizing that only one religion can ultimately be true.

Logically speaking, it can't both be true that there is one God and there are many gods; the two beliefs are mutually exclusive. Other beliefs also seem to be mutually exclusive. When believers get to heaven, will they find Jesus on the throne at the right hand of God the Father or learn that Muhammad had it right? Is the Bible, properly interpreted, the correct way to understand God, or should we study and learn the sutras of Buddhism? Is there a cyclical pattern to human existence so that souls are reincarnated into higher or lower life forms, or is human existence linear with life after death in another world? Perhaps the atheists are right, and there is no God and no reality other than the one modern science describes.

Each of these options presents a faith choice, and they cannot all be right. In fact, no more than one religion can be entirely correct. We might pick parts of each religion and create a new one, but that would be suggesting that the new one was right and the others only partially correct. Finally, if we think about religious questions deeply enough, we realize that there can be only one true religion.

Yet that feels wrong somehow. There has been so much conflict among religious groups and so much persecution and war, we fear that the claim of truth about matters of faith will cause big problems for the whole human community.

As a result, many Christians join nonreligious people in looking at all the conflict and violence, much of it having religious overtones, and saying: Why can't we all just get along together? Aren't most of our religions about love and spiritual values? How can we avoid the bad influence that religions sometimes have had?

How to View Other Religions

If we believe that only one religion can ultimately be true, we are led inevitably to a third step: deciding how, within one religion's commitments, believers should view other religions.

In the United Methodist faith tradition, for example, we start with belief in the prevenient grace of God. Every human being has received God's grace, and God is working in all our lives to bring us toward salvation. There are many valid and valuable beliefs and practices in other religions. Many religions teach moral values such as loving our neighbors, caring for the poor, respecting creation, practicing prayer, and working for the common good. We look at those beliefs and practices and say that God was at work through that other religion to help people come as close to the truth as possible, given their culture and history.

John Wesley, the founder of Methodism, approached the salvation of people outside the Christian faith by saying that God will judge us all according to how we use the grace we have been given. Thus, people raised in other religious faiths may be saved.

Wesley's view leads to a spiritual attitude of openness and curiosity. When we encounter a follower of another religion, we should be asking, "How is God's grace at work in this person's life and practice?"

Thus, when we see Muslims dedicated to prayer and fasting, we realize that we can learn from them about how God has helped to shape their religion and their culture. When we see Buddhists focus on meditation and respect for all forms of life, we can recognize the Holy Spirit at work in their religion.

Of particular importance is how Christians relate to Jews. The way that early Christianity separated from Judaism in the first century has led to a variety of misconceptions about followers of that religion. We believe that Jews remain

God's chosen people and that God continues to have a special place for them in the plan of salvation. Paul describes Gentile Christians as branches from a wild olive tree grafted on to the cultivated tree. We are dependent on our Jewish brothers and sisters in many ways. But Romans 11:26 says it clearly: "In this way, all Israel will be saved."

Thus, when Christians persecute Jews (as has happened all too often in the last two thousand years), they are not truly following Christ. Many evil things have been done in the name of Christianity.

C. S. Lewis, in the last book of the Chronicles of Narnia, describes a scene in which a soldier who was a follower of Tash made it into heaven and was surprised to see Aslan the Lion there. The soldier, who had spent his whole life following a different religion, was amazed, first, to find out the truth and, second, to be accepted into heaven though believing in a different God. Aslan told him that all the good deeds done in the name of Tash were offerings made to Aslan and that all the evil deeds done in the name of Aslan were offered to Tash.[6]

We firmly believe that God can welcome people into heaven who faithfully practice other religions. Here on earth we should offer them Christ at every opportunity, but also look for common areas of interest and concern where we can work together.

Following the terrorist attacks on September 11, 2001, many Muslims were appalled at what the terrorists had done, and they quickly condemned those actions as violating the principles of Islam. Many Christians reached out to build relationships with local Muslims. Scott was in a dialogue presentation with local Muslim leaders who emphasized the many ways in which Christianity and Islam agree about moral issues. All were clear that the war against terrorism was not a religious war but one being fought against evil persons by nations such as the United States that have many different religious groups.

Scott has often described Christian teaching as occupying the "extreme center." By that he means holding in tension two ideas that are sometimes seen as contradictory. At the very least, that effort generates intellectual tension and interesting conversation. Our attitude toward persons of other religions has some of that tension in it.

On the one hand, there are good people who believe in and follow other religions, and we should treat them with love, respect, and curiosity. We know God's grace is at work within them and they may have things to teach us about God and how to live a good life. Jesus told the parable of the good Samaritan in Luke 10:30-37. When a man was wounded and lying in a ditch, it was the Samaritan who bandaged his wounds and paid for his care. Jews despised Samaritans—one of the religious conflicts mentioned in the Bible. Yet Jesus used this example of how the two great commandments—loving God and loving your neighbor as yourself—should transcend religious animosities.

On the other hand, we believe that ultimately the world's other religions are at best incomplete and in some ways wrong. Because we are dealing with truth claims about ultimate reality, one of these religions has to be more nearly right than the others. Having said that, Christians realize that their understanding of God is incomplete. Paul wrote, "Now we see a reflection in a mirror; then we will see face-to-face. Now I know partially, but then I will know completely in the same way that I have been completely known." (1 Corinthians 13:12).

Living in the extreme center means holding both our truth claims and our love for non-Christians in productive tension. We must believe and act on both! Christians have a strong obligation both to love their neighbors and to evangelize them. In his book *The Evangelistic Love of God and Neighbor*, Scott wrote, "To evangelize non-Christian persons without loving them fully is not to evangelize them well. To love non-Christian persons without evangelizing them is not to love them well. Loving God well means loving one's non-Christian neighbor evangelistically and evangelizing one's non-Christian neighbor lovingly."[7] In this way, we can hold in tension two essential values that, considered separately and incompletely, could lead to conflict or syncretism.

Rapid Response

So, imagine yourself in a coffee shop hanging out, talking about whatever, and suddenly your non-Christian friend says, "Okay, I don't want a long complicated answer, but tell me this: How can you believe that only Christianity is true when there are all these other religions?"

You might say something like this: "I believe Christianity is true. I know that believing it is an act of faith, but picking any religion is an act of faith, or even picking no religion at all. I respect other religions, and I'm sure God can work through them all, but I've experienced God's presence through Jesus and I can't deny it. We all choose something, and I've chosen to follow Jesus."

2.
Why Is There Suffering and Evil?

2.
Why Is There Suffering and Evil?

Problems and tragedies abound in our world, and they come in a variety of ways to kill and destroy.

A woman we will call Cathy died tragically of breast cancer. She had three children, and doctors found a very aggressive form of the cancer while she was pregnant with her fourth. Cathy was a woman of strong faith who was very active in her church. She participated in Bible study, Sunday school, and weekly worship. She led a midweek children's ministry that included a choir for elementary school kids. Her main wish in fighting the cancer was to live long enough to see her children graduate from high school. To everyone's dismay, Cathy died a few years after the original diagnosis. Her early death, leaving behind the family that she loved, was a tragedy that deeply saddened all who knew her. They kept asking: Why?

Another family in a different city appeared to have it all. Frank and Margaret were successful in their careers. They lived in a nice home and were admired by all who knew them. From the outside, they were living the American dream. But Frank was a sex addict who was engaging in multiple affairs with women he barely knew. Frank knew he was violating his marriage vows and did all he could to keep his infidelity a secret from Margaret. But one day she found electronic evidence of an affair and confronted him. She thought she had been doing all that a wife could or should do to keep her husband happy. But Frank had broken his commitment, not just once but many times. Margaret found the grace to forgive Frank, and they remained married. But ten years later she discovered evidence of another affair. Frank entered therapy for sex addiction and was forced to confront his own need to do such destructive things. Both Margaret and Frank asked: Why?

In Scott's generation, everyone knows where they were on November 22, 1963, when John F. Kennedy was assassinated. In Arthur's generation, perhaps, the defining event is referred to simply as 9/11. On September 11, 2001, the towers of the World Trade Center went down and the Pentagon was attacked, killing 2,977 people.[1] At that time, few Americans had heard of Al Qaeda or knew what caused radical jihadist Muslims to attack Western countries so violently. After fourteen years of the so-called War on Terror, many people look at the bombings and atrocities and once again ask: Why?

On August 29, 2005, Hurricane Katrina made landfall in Louisiana. Though it was only a Category 3 storm by the time it hit, the storm surge forced its way into New Orleans and the surrounding area, wreaking terrible damage. Approximately 1,200 people died from the storm and related flooding, and property damage was calculated at $75 billion.[2] Many of the people who died were too poor to leave the city when the warnings sounded. When natural disasters strike, causing so much death and destruction, people ask: Why?

World War 1 started on July 28, 1914, when Austria-Hungary declared war on Serbia and then invaded. During the next four years the major European countries engaged in warfare with a technological power never before seen in human history. More than 8,500,000 soldiers died.[3] And the deaths didn't stop there. Charles Tilly, a sociologist at Columbia University, wrote of the twentieth century, "Altogether, about 100 million people died as a direct result of action by organized military units backed by one government or another over the course of the century. Most likely a comparable number of civilians died of war-induced disease and other indirect effects."[4] The twenty-first century has not seen war on this major scale, but conflicts continue. As of this writing, significant wars are taking place in Pakistan, Afghanistan, Iraq, Syria, Ukraine, and Nigeria, and the deaths multiply.

Whether from war, terrorism, illness, natural disaster, human weakness, or sheer evil, our world has no shortage of death and tragedy. And always we ask: *Why?*

The Question

When Christians gather in large groups, sometimes the leader will start a call and response with the congregation that goes like this:

Leader: "God is good."
Congregation: "All the time."
Leader: "All the time."
Congregation: "God is good."

Christians believe that a Supreme Being cares about the world and is working for the good of all creation. In 1 John 4:8 this is stated clearly and simply: "God is love." People often quote John 3:16, "God so loved the world …"

Christians are not the only ones puzzled by the presence of evil and disasters in the world. Many people of different faiths or no faith have a sense that the world is basically a good place. Yet, the data shows that death, destruction, and violence occur with frequency.

It leads us to the question: "If God is good, why is there suffering and evil in the world?"

The Traditional Christian Answer

Christians traditionally have answered this question by starting with the goodness of creation. We say that God is good all the time, and it started with God's loving act of creating the universe from nothing. God has always existed, and at some point God decided to create a world. In the first thirty-three verses of the Bible, God created the universe in seven days. Six times it says that God's creative work was "good." After creating man and woman, the last three verses of this creation account say,

> God saw everything he had made: it was supremely good.
> There was evening and there was morning: the sixth day.
> The heavens and the earth and all who live in them were

completed. On the sixth day God completed all the work that he had done, and on the seventh day God rested from all the work that he had done. (Genesis 1:31–2:2)

Christians traditionally have interpreted these verses to mean that the world was perfect at the end of the sixth day. John Wesley, writing in the eighteenth century, stated,

> The paradisiacal earth afforded a sufficiency of food for all its inhabitants, so that none of them had any need of temptation to prey upon the other. The spider was as harmless as the fly, and did not then lie in wait for blood. The weakest of them crept securely over the earth, or spread their gilded wings in the air, that waved in the breeze and glittered in the sun without any to make them afraid. Meantime the reptiles of every kind were equally harmless and more intelligent than they.[5]

The world did not have death, disease, or evil in it. It truly was paradise.

However, humanity had been created in God's own image, with free will to choose good or evil. Genesis 3 recounts the conversations between the serpent, Eve, and Adam. Eve's first mistake was in adding to what God had told Adam, claiming that she could not even touch the fruit of the tree in the middle of the garden. Then she believed the serpent rather than God and ate of the forbidden fruit. Adam followed and did the same thing. By Adam and Eve's deliberate disobedience, sin entered the world, and the whole creation fell. Humans were expelled from the garden, and disease and disaster followed. According to this traditional account, all of humanity is descended from the first two humans, whose disobedience changed everything.

Thus, the traditional answer to the origin of evil, death, and disaster is the disobedience of Adam and Eve. All human beings are born as sinners, a view called original sin. At the same time, God's love meant that God immediately set out to fix the problems caused by humans.

The Bible is an ongoing story about a loving God working to cure humanity of its sins and restore creation to its intended perfection. Humanity still retains free will and frequently rejects God's loving overtures and desires. Through it all, God never gives up. The history of the world can be recounted as creation, fall into sin, redemption, and new creation.

Today's Christian Answer

Modern Christians read the first three chapters of Genesis as powerful and true stories about the human condition, but not as a history of how the world came to be. We accept what modern science tells us about the world being millions of years old and life evolving over time.

Such scientific knowledge answers questions about how God created the world, in ways we can't expect those questions to be answered by the Bible. It is unrealistic to expect that God would have revealed such knowledge to the Hebrew people thousands of years ago. Over time, human beings have begun to figure out how God works through natural processes. Some persons have called this intellectual position theistic evolution.

As our understanding of the world has grown and we can no longer blame all bad things in this world on human sin, the question of suffering and evil is split into two questions. First, why is there suffering from natural disasters and disease? Second, why is there human evil in the world?

Disease and Natural Disaster

The question about natural disasters and disease requires that we start with a fundamental claim of Christian teaching. We believe that God is good all the time and that God created a good world. There are many occasions when we connect with the beauty of creation or the amazing complexity of the universe and know that a good and loving God must have designed and created it. The Hubble telescope has sent back pictures of other galaxies that are visually stunning and show the beauty of God's creation. The Ant Nebula, for example, is about eight thousand light years from earth, and its beauty can be viewed online at the NASA website (http://www.jpl.nasa.gov/spaceimages/details.php?id=pia04216). The amazing pictures we now get from distant galaxies reinforce the wonder expressed by Stuart Hine in his hymn, "How Great Thou Art."

O Lord my God! when I in awesome wonder
Consider all the worlds thy hands have made,
I see the stars, I hear the rolling thunder,
Thy power throughout the universe displayed.[6]

As we write this, Arthur's sister and Scott's daughter Marynell is expecting her first child. We have seen a sonogram taken at ten weeks of pregnancy, and already the shape of a baby human is visible. When new life comes into being, we praise God and are amazed at the wonderful world that God has created.

But such wonder at the goodness of creation simply sets up the problem of suffering and evil. God created magnificent clouds and weather patterns that can produce hurricanes such as Katrina, which killed so many and caused so much destruction. And sometimes precious babies die within days of birth or suffer from birth defects and diseases. How do we explain a world in which a loving God allows natural disasters and disease?

The first point in a Christian explanation is that God's creation allows for incredible complexity. Thunderstorms and violent weather play an important role in the larger ecology of the world. A forest fire causes massive destruction of trees and the deaths of animals, but it also cleanses the ecology and restores systems to balance. We do not know if it is possible for a world to exist that does not have some of these destructive forces in it. Many Christian thinkers suggest that a world as complicated as ours will inevitably have parts that appear to be destructive and yet are necessary to the working of creation as a whole.

In the powerful video "How Wolves Change Rivers," a group called Sustainable Human (sustainablehuman.me) tells the story of changes wrought by the reintroduction of wolves into Yellowstone National Park.[7] Wolves are predators, and they were hunted by the people who settled Montana. Wolves are still feared by many people, and they are disliked by those raising cattle because of the economic losses they inflict. When Yellowstone National Park was founded, there were provisions to protect the wolves. Yet they still were hunted, and the last one was killed in 1926. In 1995 and 1996, thirty-one wolves were captured in Canada and released in the park. Amazing consequences from this simple act came about. The wolves killed the deer. The deer moved away from the valleys. Vegetation increased because there were fewer deer in certain areas.

More vegetation stabilized the riverbanks and allowed the population of other animals to increase. The whole ecosystem became healthier and more stable because wolves had come back. Scientists called this kind of environmental change a trophic cascade, in which the change in a predator at the top of the food chain alters many other aspects of the environment.

A theological point that can be drawn from this situation: God created our world to have amazing complexity and delicate balances. What may look like evil—the predation of wolves upon deer and cattle—is actually an important part of the whole balance of creation. Modern science has improved our understandings of ecosystems to include the interconnections of all parts of the world. This gives strength to the Christian claim that the world is created as good, even if it involves death and destruction in certain instances.

A second reason that Christians might give for why a loving God allows natural disasters and disease is that many of God's creatures have a level of freedom that allows them to move and act on their own. Though ultimately in control of the universe, God has deliberately and creatively allowed creatures to move and act independently. A few years ago, a woman unbuckled her seat belt to do something for her children in the backseat, and at that moment a deer ran in front of their car. Because the car was traveling at a high speed, she was thrown through the windshield and died. This tragedy seemed senseless, and people asked "Why did God allow this to happen?" It seems clear that God did not will her death. Instead, her decision to care for her children in this way coupled with the deer's impulse to cross the highway created the situation that led to her death. God created a world in which creatures make choices, and sometimes there are tragic results.

Human Evil

The problem of human evil has a simpler (if more troubling) answer: humans are given the capacity for freedom and with that freedom choose to commit evil. Christianity teaches that all human beings are sinners. One of the mysteries of human existence is our propensity to sin. All human beings are sinners as is expressed in Psalm 51. The heading of this Psalm says "A Psalm of David, when the prophet Nathan came to him just after he had been with Bathsheba." According to the account in 2 Samuel 11, David (who had many wives) saw Bathsheba bathing and desired her. He had sex with her and she got pregnant. David then arranged for her husband, Uriah, to die in battle so that he would be free to marry her, which he did. This psalm expresses David's remorse after the Nathan confronted him for his evil deed.

> Have mercy on me, God, according to your faithful love!
>> Wipe away my wrongdoings according to your great
>> compassion!
> Wash me completely clean of my guilt;
>> purify me from my sin!
> Because I know my wrongdoings,
>> my sin is always right in front of me.
> I've sinned against you—you alone.
>> I've committed evil in your sight.
> That's why you are justified when you render your verdict,
>> completely correct when you issue your judgment.
> Yes, I was born in guilt, in sin,
>> from the moment my mother conceived me.
> And yes, you want truth in the most hidden places;
>> you teach me wisdom in the most secret space.
>
> Purify me with hyssop and I will be clean;
>> wash me and I will be whiter than snow.
> Let me hear joy and celebration again;
>> let the bones you crushed rejoice once more.
> Hide your face from my sins;
>> wipe away all my guilty deeds!
> Create a clean heart for me, God;
>> put a new, faithful spirit deep inside me!
> Please don't throw me out of your presence;
>> please don't take your holy spirit away from me.
> Return the joy of your salvation to me
>> and sustain me with a willing spirit.
> Then I will teach wrongdoers your ways,
>> and sinners will come back to you.

One of the crucial points in the psalm is the claim that he was born a sinner. All human beings struggle with evil desires that go against God's laws. Christians also know that God's grace is active in our lives before we are ever aware of it. So every human being has the freedom to either follow the evil impulses we are born with, or to follow God's leading to obey God's laws and follow the moral path.

It is not hard to make the case that all human beings are sinners. The reality is that too many people ignore God's grace in their lives and choose the evil paths. Sometimes evil acts are committed unintentionally. Most of us can point to times when we were trying to do the right thing, but we did not understand all of the factors in the situation and we ended up causing great pain and suffering to others. At the other end of the spectrum, there are people who are so filled with hatred that they set out to intentionally inflict harm on others.

The question that needs an answer is this: Why does God allow such sinful activity by human beings? The question goes back to the Bible's claim that human beings were created in God's own image, with the freedom to choose between good and evil. Should God have created robots? Is God's creation truly good when human beings have the capacity for murder, hatred, oppression, and all other forms of evil? God clearly chose to allow for human freedom while knowing that there would be negative consequences. Perhaps it is our capacity for evil that makes the moments when we choose good so important.

Suffering Redeemed

Suffering provides an opportunity for God's grace to be at work. This is true of broken human relationships, pain caused by human evil, and the destruction wreaked by natural disasters. Ultimately we must admit that the questions we bring to such events probably will not be answered to our satisfaction. We look for meaning and purpose behind these events, and often there is none. If we consult Scripture, however, Jesus redirects our thinking to the response we are called to make. Many situations that involve suffering also create opportunities for God's love and compassion to be shown. Here is one example of Jesus' response:

> As Jesus walked along, he saw a man who was blind from birth. Jesus' disciples asked, "Rabbi, who sinned so that he was born blind, this man or his parents?" Jesus answered, "Neither he nor his parents. This happened so that God's mighty works might be displayed in him. While it's daytime, we must do the works of him who sent me. Night is coming when no one can work. While I am in the world, I am the light of the world." After he said this, he spit on the ground, made mud with the saliva, and smeared the mud on the man's eyes. Jesus said to him, "Go, wash in the pool of Siloam" (this word means sent). So the man went away and washed. When he returned, he could see. (John 9:1-7)

This approach informed the thinking of Nathan Kilbourne, pastor of the Vilonia United Methodist Church in Arkansas. In February 2014, he preached on the Christian response to suffering from disasters, saying,

> What does humanity have to offer in light of tragedy? Can we stop it? Why is there evil in the world? Why suffering? Such questions often lead us to doubt God and one another. Yet, for instance if a tornado hits and there is no God, then what answer is there to evil or suffering? What meaning and purpose? Life is just tragic and terror is always on the horizon. I would rather live in the world that has a possibility of God then one that has none, particularly one like this where evil rears its ugly head so often and is just merely a "fact of life." Life then truly becomes meaningless, hopeless, and depressing. Yet with the possibility of God comes the possibility of meaning, purpose, and hope being found in the midst of tragedy and suffering. Albeit we are still left with questions, it is more of a world worth living in than the other option.[8]

Six weeks later a tornado struck his town, killing nine people and destroying many buildings, including the Vilonia United Methodist Church. The Sunday following the tornado, Kilbourne preached on Luke 24:32, where the disciples asked, "Were not our hearts burning within us?" (NRSV). Christ was present on the road to Emmaus even if they did not recognize him. Similarly, when people go through tragedies such as the tornado, Christ is present but the people involved may not see him there. The Christian perspective is to help people experience the presence and love of Christ even in the most difficult situations.

Thus, many Christians find themselves involved in disaster relief operations. They respond to human need by feeding people, clearing away debris, and assisting rebuilding efforts. Just as Jesus said about the man born blind, the right question is how God's grace can be made manifest in the situations where we find ourselves.

Ultimately, if we believe in God there may be no satisfactory answer to the problem of evil. Atheists see a meaningless universe, where there is no purpose and the world is governed by random chance. But for those who believe in God, there will always be a sense of mystery about why human evil is permitted, along with disease and natural disasters.

Natalie Sleeth's husband, Ron, was nearing death, and she turned her considerable talent for music to a poetic statement of faith in her inspiring "Hymn of Promise." This beautiful hymn expressed her faith, concluding with these lines:

> In our death, a resurrection; at the last, a victory,
> Unrevealed until its season, something God alone can see.[9]

We human beings, limited and finite as we are, do not have all the answers. We have far more questions than knowledge, but we trust that our lives are in God's hands whatever happens.

Rapid Response

You are in the coffee shop hanging out with one of your non-Christian friends, who says, "Okay, I don't want a long complicated answer, but tell me this: If God is so good, how come there is so much bad stuff in the world? If there is a God, God must cause evil, right?"

You might respond, "I don't have all the answers, but I know that God is loving and that God works for good in all situations. In the worst times of my life, I have experienced the love of God in multiple ways that have helped me make it through. I know there are disasters and evil things in this world, but God is a force for good. I'm a Christian because I want to be part of that force for good in the world."

3.
How Can I Believe in Science and Creation?

3.

How Can I Believe in Science and Creation?

Science is all about asking questions to get data—observable evidence that allows us humans to understand and make predictions about the world. As the sciences have developed over the past few hundred years, we have discovered more and more about our amazing world. Powerful telescopes have allowed us to see solar systems in the darkest parts of our night sky. Electron microscopes enable us to understand the building blocks of our bodies and the atoms that make up our world. Particle accelerators send those building blocks crashing against each other in order to gather more data about the creation of the universe. Scientists have shown that gathering and analyzing data is one effective way to eliminate false beliefs and advance human knowledge.

Inevitably, however, scientists draw false conclusions along the way. Prominent scientists during the eighteenth century, for example, believed that draining some blood from a person's body was a good way to remove illness from the body. In fact, if you are looking for scientists who believe crazy things, you can always find them. "There are many hypotheses in science which are wrong," the astrophysicist Carl Sagan once said. "That's perfectly all right: it's the aperture to finding out what's right. Science is a self-correcting process."[1] Scientists constantly ask questions. The goal is to ask the right questions so they get enough data to ask the next question. Scientists expect truth to be found in hard data that results from empirical evidence.

People of faith, though, believe that trusting only the physical world is too limited a way to view existence. In fact, many of our most important questions are outside the scope of science, such as questions about why we are here and how we are supposed to live our lives. Science and religion are not by definition opposites, and yet that is often how scientists and Christians approach each other.

The Question

This divide became apparent to Arthur in the fall of 2002 during his first semester at the University of Kansas, when he was involved in a religious group on campus and at the same time was taking an introductory biology class. The basis of the biology class was evolutionary theory—that all living creatures are descended from prior beings that over millions of years evolved to the current forms. For example, study of the bone structures of birds indicates that they were ancestors of dinosaurs. Similarly, fossil evidence shows human ancestors that were not *Homo sapiens*. Though technically evolution is a theory, the data for this approach is overwhelming.

At the same time he was studying evolution in biology class, Arthur had friends at a conservative Christian religious organization that semester and began attending worship services with them. At a Bible study, one of the leaders criticized science teachers who he said were challenging Christianity by teaching evolution. Arthur described some of the concepts presented in his biology class, and after the Bible study one of the leaders pulled him aside and invited him to a special gathering where a graduate of MIT was speaking to "debunk" the theories of evolution. When Arthur got to the gathering, the speaker made some science-based arguments, but the most significant part of his speech was that "The devil is on campus! He is using science to tell young people lies about God."

It was a vivid illustration of the divide between science and religion. In biology class, religious questions and truths were not allowed. In the church group, the science teachers were called liars and tools of the devil.

The idea that science and religion are opposed has persisted well into the twenty-first century. A seventh-grader from Arthur's church asked her small group leader, "What about God and evolution? We talk about that in science class…" Her expectation was that there inevitably would be a conflict between teachings about her God and the lessons of her science class.

Are science and faith mutually exclusive? Faith raises questions about science and the creation of the world, and science raises questions about faith and how we got here. So, is it possible for us to accept both science and faith? Does belief in one lessen the validity of the other?

Faith Versus Science

As science has developed, it has won major battles against faith, minimizing areas of the church's authority. One of the most celebrated examples was the trial of Galileo Galilei. The church had held a position called geocentrism, or belief that the sun revolved around the earth, which was supported in part by a literal reading of 1 Chronicles 16:30: "Tremble before him, all the earth! Yes, he set the world firmly in place; it won't be shaken." This Scripture turned out to be great theology but horrible science.

Galileo, the great scientist, asked the right questions, gathered data through the use of newly developed telescopes and observation of the tides, and determined that the earth's location was not fixed. Based on the data, he determined that the earth moved around the sun, a belief known as heliocentrism. Because he followed the data rather than theology, Galileo was tried and convicted of heresy and punished by house arrest until his death.

Galileo may have lost the battle, but he won the war. Today, the movement of the earth is accepted and understood even by persons of faith. In 1992, Pope John Paul II admitted that the Roman Catholic Church made a mistake in condemning Galileo over 300 years earlier. Given today's understanding, what is the lesson of Galileo? Is it that scientists will be proven right in the end? Is it just a matter of waiting for science to prove faith wrong?

Another celebrated example was the so-called Scopes Monkey Trial, which took place in 1925 in the town of Dayton, Tennessee. This trial pitted the prevailing scientific opinion—belief in evolution—against a traditional and literal understanding of Scripture—belief in creationism. Though technically the creationists won the trial, their position was discredited in the wider culture.

The battle goes on today, and the real tragedy is that, as Arthur discovered, few good places exist to ask hard questions about faith to persons of science or to ask hard questions about science to persons of faith.

Many young people have already made their decision. A Barna study in 2007 found that 72 percent of young people ages 16–29 outside the church claim that Christians are "out of touch with reality."[2] An important reason for this view is because the church is seen as anti-science; some even believe that science removes the need for God. Does it have to be this way?

A Christian Answer

Our conviction is that the fight between science and religion is a false argument. Belief in one does not necessitate rejection of the other, even though that has become the standard view during the last few centuries. The fact is that many Christians embrace the findings of science; this was true even in the early church.

Consider evolution. Long before Charles Darwin, some Christian theologians rejected a literal interpretation of the creation accounts in Genesis. Origen, a third-century theologian, wrote:

> Who is so foolish as to suppose that God, after the manner of a husbandman, planted a paradise in Eden, towards the east, and placed in it a tree of life, visible and palpable, so that one tasting of the fruit by the bodily teeth obtained life?... And if God is said to walk in the paradise in the evening, and Adam to hide himself under a tree, I do not suppose that anyone doubts that these things figuratively indicate certain mysteries, the history having taken place in appearance, *and not literally* (emphasis added).[3]

And in the fifth century, the great theologian St. Augustine wrote:

> It is a disgraceful and dangerous thing for an infidel to hear a Christian, presumably giving the meaning of Holy Scripture,

talking non-sense on [scientific] topics.... How are they going to believe [Scripture] in matters concerning the resurrection of the dead, the hope of eternal life, and the kingdom of heaven, when they think their pages are full of falsehoods on facts which they themselves have learn[ed] from experience and the light of reason?... We should remember that Scripture, even in its obscure passages, has been written to nourish our souls.[4]

In other words, Scripture contains "all things necessary to salvation,"[5] not all things necessary for biology or physics classes. We do damage to religion when we treat Scripture like a scientific textbook, just as we do damage to science when we expect it to answer questions about a creator. Scientists and theologians often talk past one another because they are asking different questions. At their best, both science and religion lead us toward different kinds of truth.

To see how these differences play out, let's take a look at some of the key issues in the conversation between religion and science.

Origin of the Cosmos: The Big Bang and Genesis 1:1

We begin at the beginning: the origin of the universe. Both Christians and scientists agree that the universe had a beginning—that the world was not always as it is now, and that once there was a time when the universe as we know it did not exist. Current scientific data indicates that that moment (often called the singularity) occurred 13.7 billion years ago with a massive explosion that has been called the big bang. The fact that there was a beginning was not always so clear in the scientific community. Sir James Jeans, a scientist and agnostic mason in the early twentieth century, attempted to prove that there was no singular moment of creation; instead, he proposed a steady state of continual creation. In the years since, however, the evidence has lined up with what Christians and Jews have always believed, that there was a beginning.

This is how the Bible starts: "In the beginning God created the heavens and the earth" (Genesis 1:1 NIV). The assumption, of course, is that before the heavens and the earth existed, there was God. This belief is outside the scope of scientific inquiry. By the very nature of the discipline, science can only make claims based upon observable evidence, and yet Scripture (and nearly all religions) makes a claim about a being who existed before observable evidence existed. Scientists, for example, are able to look at light from distant stars, analyze the elements, and work to recreate the first moments after the big bang. All the evidence that exists is from the moments after the big bang. That's why it is called the singularity: it is that from which everything came. Analyzing evidence of the millisecond before that moment is impossible, because there is nothing to analyze. When Christians say God existed before the universe was created and scientists say there is no evidence for it, they both could be telling the truth.

Religion, as a revelation, is a connecting point between normal human experience and something outside the physical reality of this world. Science, in contrast, can explain when and how the world was created, but that explanation only leads to more questions. What caused the singularity and the big bang? If nothing existed before that moment, then how did it start? Is it possible that religion has access to a different truth? How could it be that a singular moment billions of years ago could result in life, love, hope, and family if nothing existed to shape it? This line of questioning is what Werner Heisenberg (twentieth-century theologian and winner of the Nobel Prize in physics) meant when he said, "The first gulp from the glass of natural sciences will turn you into an atheist, but at the bottom of the glass God is waiting for you."[6]

The more questions we ask about the world, the more we see that every system will, in the end, require some point of belief beyond what we can prove. The foundation and fabric of our world urge us toward a belief in something we cannot see. They might even lead us to the entity that made it: God.

Sustaining of the Universe: God or the Multiverse?

One illustration that science needs belief in something beyond the provable is the idea of a multiverse (short for multiple universes), a concept often encountered in science fiction narratives. One example is the television show *Stargate SG-1*, in which earth explorers travel to other worlds. In one episode, an explorer finds a device that sends him to an alternate universe, where things are similar to ours but with small differences. This alternate universe represents a branch of reality in which people have made different choices. By the end of the episode he is able to return with a critical piece of information to save his original universe. Though there is no evidence or suggestion that travel between universes will ever actually be possible, the basic idea of multiple universes is currently being considered by many high-profile physicists and cosmologists.

Why should this matter to us? Because the idea of multiple universes tends to downplay the importance of God's existence. Believers often maintain that the uniqueness of creation and life in this universe points to a creator. But infinite parallel universes would mean the existence of so many worlds that life such as ours is not so much special as inevitable. Humanity would not have to be designed but simply be the lucky beneficiaries of living in the right section of the right universe.

Scientists do not all agree that the multiverse exists. Of those who do believe it, there is not a consensus about the format of the multiverse or even the numbers of alternative universes. This lack of consistency within the scientific community, though, has not kept the idea from gaining traction in sci-fi shows and even mainstream media outlets. In an interview with John Oliver (formerly of *The Daily Show*), Stephen Hawking made this idea much more mainstream. John said to Stephen, "You've stated that you believe there could be an infinite number of parallel universes. Does that mean that there is a universe out there where I am smarter than you?" Stephen replied, "Yes, and also a universe where you're funny."[7] As humorous as Hawking might be, it is important to realize that this proposal of Hawking and others appears to be just as unprovable as God. Paul Davies, in an article published in the *New York Times*, wrote:

> For a start, how is the existence of the other universes to be tested? To be sure, all cosmologists accept that there are some regions of the universe that lie beyond the reach of our telescopes, but somewhere on the slippery slope between that and the idea that there are an infinite number of universes, credibility reaches a limit. As one slips down that slope, more and more must be accepted on faith, and less and less is open

to scientific verification. Extreme multiverse explanations are therefore reminiscent of theological discussions. Indeed, invoking an infinity of unseen universes to explain the unusual features of the one we do see is just as ad hoc as invoking an unseen Creator. The multiverse theory may be dressed up in scientific language, but in essence it requires the same leap of faith.[8]

If Davies is correct, any statement about the creation or fundamental underpinnings of our universe requires faith of some kind—either in a multiverse that makes the oddities and idiosyncrasies of our world possible or a creator that initiated the big bang and shaped our world to be the way it is today, including life as we know it.

The Creation and Development of Life

Life on this planet was not inevitable. In fact, the odds that this particular world would develop into the beautiful, complex, and diverse biosphere we see were miniscule. Forrest Pool, a member of Arthur's small group, had his first child this year. After holding his healthy baby boy, Forrest remarked, "I don't know how anyone cannot believe in God after holding their own child." His awe and wonder were even more appropriate when we consider that in addition to that one child being born, the miracle of birth happens over and over again in exactly the right way.

Is God the best explanation for our miraculous existence? Or is it simply because there are so many galaxies and solar systems that contain the building blocks of life that one inevitably was going to produce it without any need for God? Is our existence a blessing or sheer luck? In his book *The Blind Watchmaker*, Richard Dawkins discusses the idea that "given enough time, a monkey bashing away at random on a typewriter could produce all the works of Shakespeare."[9] Similarly, perhaps life is the creation not of an intentional design (by God) but of so many galaxies and worlds that some would inevitably produce life. On the other side is Forrest Pool's statement that life, instead of being the result of randomness, is a gift of God. After all, the first chapters of Genesis start with the creation not only of the world but of humanity. In

Genesis 2:7 we read that "the LORD God formed the human from the topsoil of the fertile land and blew life's breath into his nostrils. The human came to life."

The difference between randomness and design in the explanations for life is most clearly seen in the debate over the accepted scientific principle of evolution. "Biological evolution, simply put, is descent with modification."[10] In other words, the concept of evolution explains the diversity of life forms through randomness and natural selection as opposed to design. The story doesn't begin (as it does in the Bible) with two fully formed humans, but rather describes humans who have developed over time from one common ancestral tree.

Charles Darwin, the nineteenth-century formulator of this theory, wrote, "Therefore I should infer from analogy that probably all the organic beings which have ever lived on this earth have descended from some one primordial form, into which life was first breathed."[11] Over the years since Darwin formulated his theory, other scientists have proposed and found overwhelming evidence that all living creatures are linked at the very fundamental nature of our DNA because we are all descended some 3.5–3.8 billion years ago from some single-celled organism.

The challenge for Christians is that a strict reading of Scripture contradicts this story. If Genesis is to be taken literally, we find that the world was created about six thousand years ago. In fact, Archbishop James Ussher's seventeenth-century attempt to determine a creation chronology based on Scripture indicated that the world was created on Sunday, October 23, 4004 B.C.

But this contradiction is only a challenge if Genesis is meant to be understood literally. Consider the story of Cain. The first two people, Adam and Eve, bore two sons, Cain and Abel. In a fit of rage, Cain killed Abel and then was banished. At this point in the story, only three people existed in the entire world—Adam, Eve, and Cain—and yet this is Cain's response:

> Cain said to the LORD, "My punishment is more than I can bear. Now that you've driven me away from the fertile land and I am hidden from your presence, I'm about to become a roving nomad on the earth, and anyone who finds me will kill me" (Genesis 4:13-14).

God then placed a mark upon Cain so that no one who found him would assault him. But who were all those other people? In verse 17, Cain found a wife; where did the wife come from? Maybe these and other questions indicate that Genesis is not meant to be taken literally. The story in Scripture requires us to fill in the gaps. Is it possible that the gaps in Scripture can allow for evolution?

When scientists and Christians talk about the origins of the universe, there is a fundamental difference in their lines of questioning. The primary questions of Scripture are who and why, and then to a lesser extent what. Genesis tells us that God created the heavens and the earth and even the animals on that earth. The rest of Scripture tells us that God is love and created the world and humanity out of that love. On the other hand, Darwin was asking what processes created the diversity that exists in life all around us. These are fundamentally different and not necessarily competing areas of interest.

What if the fight over the last two hundred years is pointless, and we discover that there are amazing commonalities between the findings of science and the story of life found in Scripture? Genesis 1 describes the creation in a step-by-step process; science tells us that all living things evolved. Scripture says there is a creator who made this world so we might develop and grow; science has determined that all humanity has a common ancestral tree, that in scientific terms we are all connected. Genesis tells us to take care of the earth because it is a gift, and Jesus made it clear that everyone on earth is our neighbor; science posits that we are all connected.

Maybe, finally, this is where we will find unity between science and religion: the miracle of life.

Wisdom in Both

Science is all about asking questions to get data and find answers, but life is about more than the physical processes of our world. Forrest Pool found that out. Forrest is an educated and successful man. He can tell you, in scientific terms, how his new child came to be. But the knowledge of how children are created does not decrease the amazing fact that it happens.

Both science and faith are necessary for wisdom in this modern world. A religionless view denies part of our identity and fails to answer questions of meaning and purpose. Science can help us understand the building blocks of the universe moments after it was created but cannot answer the question of why it was created or who might have created it. Science cannot provide many answers at all about some of the most important things in life, such as hope, sacrifice, and love. These are the domain of religion.

Do we want to live in a world without religion? A religionless world would not hear that all humans are made in the image of God, that God loves us, or that we all have value. A religionless world would never hear the message to turn the other cheek or to love our neighbor as ourselves. A religionless world would never be told the idea that life can exist after death or that hope is always justified. Do we want that kind of world?

On the other hand, do we want to live in a world without science? Do we want a world with no antibiotics or computers, no airplanes or cell phones? Do we want a world without progress or understanding of how things work? We are healthier and more knowledgeable people because we have science. Many religious people who dismiss scientific thought when it contradicts Scripture will go to the doctor when they are sick.

A world without science would mean rejecting truths that are staring us in the face. For example, a college student, clinging to the idea that the earth is only six thousand years old, once tried to convince Arthur that dinosaur bones were "the devil's handiwork trying to get us to stray from God and believe in evolution." At that same student's college, dinosaur bones were on display in the natural history museum as evidence that life existed millions of years ago. Some Christians say they stand for truth and yet deny scientific truth for which there is overwhelming evidence. As a result, many people outside the church have become wary of trusting religion, seeing it as the realm of the uneducated and ignorant.

Humanity needs both religion and science. The wise path is trusting that a synthesis exists, even if we are too limited see it fully. Theologians and scientists are for the most part asking different questions, and neither ought to dismiss the other. In the words of Werner Heisenberg,

> In the history of science, ever since the famous Galileo affair, it has repeatedly been claimed that scientific truth

cannot be reconciled with the religious interpretation of the world. Although I am now convinced that scientific truth is unassailable in its own field, I have never found it possible to dismiss the content of religious thinking as simply part of an outmoded phase in the consciousness of mankind, a part we shall have to give up from now on. Thus in the course of my life I have repeatedly been compelled to ponder on the relationship of these two regions of thought, for I have never been able to doubt the reality of that to which they point.[12]

Rapid Response

In a coffee shop your non-Christian friend says, "Okay, I don't want a long complicated answer, but tell me this: How can you be a faithful Christian and still believe in modern science when the Bible teaches that the world was created six thousand years ago?"

You might say, "The difference between science and the Bible is that they are asking different questions. The Bible doesn't teach that the world was created six thousand years ago; it teaches that God created the heavens and the earth, and science by its nature has no means to test for that. The people who wrote the Bible, living only a few centuries after Jesus, were more interested in the fact of God creating the universe than in how God might have done it."

4.
How Can I Believe
in a God I Can't Prove?

4.
How Can I Believe
in a God I Can't Prove?

God's existence is not a matter of facts or data. This is why religion requires faith; God cannot be proven by physical evidence. As the author of Hebrews writes, "Faith is the reality of what we hope for, the proof of what we don't see" (Hebrews 11:1). The earliest Christians may have had something resembling proof, as they claimed to have seen Jesus resurrected from the dead, but every Christian since that unique moment in history worships a God they cannot see or touch. In fact, nearly all religions share in common beliefs about God, and none of those beliefs can be proved by data.

Our modern-day emphasis on proof and data leads many to reject a belief in God altogether. Richard Dawkins and Stephen Hawking, notably intelligent scientists, flatly reject the idea that God exists. The public nature of their rejection creates an impression among some that faith in God will diminish as intelligence increases. As pastors, we have occasionally heard various people described as "too smart to go to church." Is that possible? Is religion the arena for those who lack intelligence? Or, the better question: Is it foolish to believe in something you cannot prove?

In C. S. Lewis's novel *That Hideous Strength*, we meet a character named Andrew MacPhee who might have asked that question. MacPhee, a noted scientist who refuses to believe in God, says, "If anything wants Andrew MacPhee to believe in its existence, I'll be obliged if it will present itself in full daylight, with a sufficient number of witnesses present, and not get shy if you hold up a camera or a thermometer."[1]

In our years of ministry, we have run across numerous people who had that same mind-set. One such person came to church only because his wife believed in God, and they had made a promise to attend church as a condition of their marriage. He didn't believe in God, because he refused to believe in something he could not prove. In the couple's premarital counseling, it became clear that they had spent hours trying to convince each other that they were wrong. Such conversations rarely are effective, because neither side has real data to back up its position. This is true even for the most brilliant of atheists and theologians; neither Stephen Hawking nor the pope can definitively prove or disprove God by using data.

Most of the information available about God isn't about God at all but instead centers around the actions of those who follow God. One of the most public and prolific writers on this point is the late Christopher Hitchens, who wrote the book *God Is Not Great*, which had the very telling subtitle: *How Religion Poisons Everything*. Hitchens's basic argument is that religion is dangerous, and those who follow God do horrible things, such as Muslim extremists or Christianity's own Crusaders and Inquisitors. Debating the actions of believers is a standard conversation point when atheists and religious people debate God. This entire conversation is misguided. Both atheists and persons of faith have the capacity for greatness as well as depravity, and neither response has any effect on whether or not there is a God.

This chapter is intended to help clarify conversations such as these. In books, movies, and everyday conversations, we often debate the existence of God, and in our culture it often is done badly. Popular works by atheists in the past few decades—such as the Hitchens book or Richard Dawkins's *The God Delusion*—are interesting to read but fail because they lack a real understanding of God. By that, we mean that people of faith read these books and think, "Well, I don't believe in that God either." Both faith and atheism would be better served if authors and commentators had a better understanding of God and acknowledged that if we are to believe anything at all, then we must believe something that we cannot prove.

God and No-God

God as a concept is easier to understand when we consider its opposite: No-God. No-God is a belief that nothing exists outside our material world, and everything that exists is the consequence of chance and randomness. We exist, but that existence is not purposeful. Things such as love, which seem sacred and special, are merely chemical reactions in the brain. The world is not necessarily meaningless, but it has only the meaning we ascribe to it for the short time we exist here on earth. Everything good and bad in the universe came from nothing, and one day it will revert to nothing.

Is No-God even logically possible? Could all that exists come from nothing? Such a theory seems to violate one of our most basic expectations of the world, that everything comes from something. One leading scientist believes that it is logically possible: Lawrence Krauss, a physics professor at Arizona State University, who recently wrote a book titled *A Universe from Nothing: Why There Is Something Rather Than Nothing*. In an interview with Stephen Colbert, Krauss stated, "Nothing is unstable.... Empty space is a boiling, bubbling brew of virtual particles popping in and out of existence." The dialogue between Krauss and Colbert is helpful:

Colbert: [You are saying that] in some theoretical end space before the moment of creation, there can be no time and no space and no energy and suddenly from nowhere and from nothing comes something and somewhere... .

Krauss: And what is remarkable is that it is possible without any supernatural shenanigans.... It doesn't have to be an attack on your God.

Colbert: But that's all you've done, you've attacked my God for the last six minutes.

Krauss: No, no, no ... all I've said is you don't need him.[2]

This is the crux of the No-God proposal: that God as a concept is unnecessary (and sometimes unhelpful). All of existence—solar systems, life, civilization, love, hope, and everything else in the universe—can be explained by the material world and the laws of physics. Everything exists due to chance and randomness. No-God means that the book that you are reading now and the thoughts going through your head and the love you have for your family are all artifacts of the material world, which at the beginning emerged from nothing with no purpose.

The transition from a belief in No-God to a belief in any god is a more significant philosophical shift than many atheists understand. In the debates on this topic, occasionally you hear someone say or imply that the world has dismissed thousands of gods over its history and that one more is no big deal. Twentieth-century author and historian Stephen Roberts was quoted as saying, "I contend that we are both atheists, I just believe in one fewer god than you do. When you understand why you dismiss all the other possible gods, you will understand why I dismiss yours." Roberts's argument is that just as Christians dismiss the ancient Greek god Zeus, so he dismisses the God of Christianity. This idea demonstrates a fundamental lack of understanding about what religious people mean by God.

God is the infinite creator and sustainer of all that is and was and will be. This is the definition of God in both Western and Eastern religions, though these religions differ in their beliefs about how God engages in history. Whatever their differences, all these religions agree that the primary nature of God is outside all that has been caused and made into existence. For example, Christianity's greatest proclamation about the nature of God is found in the Nicene Creed, which begins like this:

> We believe in one God, the Father, the Almighty, maker of heaven and earth, of all that is, seen and unseen. We believe in one Lord, Jesus Christ, the only Son of God, eternally begotten of the Father, God from God, Light from Light, true God from true God, begotten, not made, of one Being with the Father; through him all things were made.[3]

The nature of God as outside and beyond the created universe is not unique to Christianity. In his book *The Experience of God*, David Bentley Hart argues that "no one really acquainted with the metaphysical and spiritual claims of major theistic faiths can fail to notice that on a host of fundamental philosophical issues, and especially on the issue of how divine transcendence should be understood, the areas of accord are quite vast."[4] Hart argues that this statement is true for the major Western faiths of Judaism, Christianity, and Islam as well as for the Eastern religions of Hinduism, Sikhism, various pagan religions, and even some Buddhist communities. The fundamental idea of God is consistent across religions.

That's Not My God

Here are four claims that demonstrate people are not talking about the same God that Christians (and other religions) believe in:

- Any claim that science has disproven God. Science deals with what is known and material, and God exists outside that sphere. God cannot fit into a beaker; if people of faith are right, God made the beaker, and though God can enter into this world he cannot be limited to it.
- Any claim that God has become irrelevant because we now understand the world. Traditionally, this claim is known as the God of the Gaps theory—that God's importance is shrinking as we learn more about our world. For example, weather and luck, which traditionally were seen as controlled by the gods, can be now be understood as predictable weather patterns and the effect of statistical chance in an unpredictable world. This knowledge might prove the mechanisms of the world but not its author.
- Any claim that differences in theology among religions mean there cannot be a God. The various religions actually have a high proportion of agreement about the basic logic pertaining to God. Differences about application do not go to the root core of the logic.
- Any claim that the actions of religious people prove there is no God. Such statements may be relevant to the effectiveness of religion or the goodness of religious people, but not to the proof of a God. God is, by definition, more expansive than the actions of anything within creation.

The Idea of God

The idea of God is easier to explain than a proof of God. As we grow up asking questions about God, we hope for scientific proof, thinking that somehow if God exists there must be a way to demonstrate it. Is such a proof possible? Not if God is truly God. So what is the point of trying to prove God? One benefit of trying is to highlight the relative strengths and weaknesses of the three general philosophical positions on the existence of God: theism, atheism, and agnosticism.

Theism is any belief in God. It encompasses a wide variety of religions and spiritualities. This belief, often called faith, does not require scientific proof; in fact, by definition such proof does not exist. As the author of Hebrews points out, faith for the theist is often its own proof: "Faith is the reality of what we hope for, the proof of what we don't see" (Hebrews 11:1). Living a life of faith is accepting that proof of God is at some level unnecessary, even impossible.

Atheism is the belief that no god exists. Most people reject some god, but atheists reject all gods. While Christians would say that Zeus is not God, atheists reject the concept of any greater being. The challenge for atheism is that, like theism, it too cannot be scientifically proven. Put another way, atheism calls for as much "faith" or belief without proof as any religion does.

Agnosticism is the third option, when a person refuses to choose between theism and atheism. Normally this refusal to choose comes from a commitment to proof. Since both theism and atheism lack scientific proof, the most logical data-based position is to refrain from making a judgment. The challenge is that agnosticism is limited in its ability to make any statement other than doubt. Agnosticism is logically consistent, but as an alternative philosophy it lacks the ability to propose a way of life and ignores the logic of God that is expressed consistently across religions.

If nobody has data about God, and if scientific proofs of God are impossible, then what kinds of logic or proofs could there possibly be for God? Quite a few, actually. People of faith have a long history of attempting to prove God. No one has developed an equation of God as self-evident as 2+2=4, but people have cited good reasons for being theists and for having faith that is neither crazy nor anti-intellectual.

Proofs of God

Let's consider arguments made in the thirteenth century by Thomas Aquinas, one of the church's greatest theologians. In his legendary work *Summa Theologica*, Aquinas walked through five proofs that for the last eight hundred years have been influential and important in this conversation.

As we approach the proofs, we must first understand their role in Aquinas's work and understanding of the world. Though these proofs are powerful and often quoted, Aquinas never intended them to be the foundation of someone's faith, since in his eyes only God could be the foundation of faith. Instead, the proofs were meant to explain the nature of God and to explore the necessary role of God in creation.

The five proofs are not separate and independent but rather building blocks of a complete argument for God. This building-block feature is easiest to understand in the first three proofs, since functionally they are the same argument written in three different ways; all three can be summed up as infinite regression arguments.

1. The Argument of the Unmoved Mover

In the unmoved mover argument, Aquinas wants us to consider motion. Something that moves had to be set in motion. If you see a car moving down the road, you know that something made that car move. If you see a log on fire in a fireplace, you know that something happened to move that log from being cold to being on fire.

The same argument can be made for creation itself. Our world exists and is moving; something must have caused that movement. Whatever caused that movement was in turn caused by something, which was caused by something else, which was caused by something else. The process can't go on forever; something had to start the world in movement, and we realize that all movement had to be started by something outside that process. Hence there must be an unmoved mover, and this we call God.

2. The Argument of the First Cause

Similar to the unmoved mover, the first cause proof relies on the ultimate regression argument, but it starts from the logical point that something that exists cannot cause itself. You cannot have birthed yourself because that means you existed before you were born. There must be something before you that caused you to exist. The same is true for the universe: there must be something that was the first cause of all that exists, and this we call God.

3. The Argument from Contingency

Everything in nature either exists or doesn't exist. A tree can exist now, but when it dies it will no longer exist, and there was a time before the tree when the tree did not exist. This is true for almost everything in the universe: there was a time before it existed when nothing existed. The key point from Aquinas: "Therefore, if at one time nothing was in existence, it would have been impossible for anything to have begun to exist; and thus now even nothing would be in existence—which is absurd." Because we exist now, we know that before everything in the universe existed there could not have been nothing. God's existence is necessary if our existence is ever to be.

These first three arguments—the Unmoved Mover, the First Cause, and Contingency—are infinite regression arguments. In order for a universe with movements, causes, and creations to exist, there must be something that moved others, that was the first cause, and that was able to create finite beings. All these arguments directly relate to the debate between Stephen Colbert and Lawrence Krauss at the beginning of this chapter. Krauss argued that God is intellectually unnecessary because "empty space is complicated. It is a boiling brew of virtual particles that pop in and out of existence in a time so short we cannot see them directly." In essence, Krauss was rejecting Aquinas by saying that something comes from nothing all the time and therefore there is no need for an unmoved mover or a first cause or a necessary being. What it really demonstrates is that Krauss misunderstood Aquinas and the fundamental logic of God. Virtual particles coming from nothing in empty space is not proof that there isn't a God, but proof that empty space isn't actually empty. Aquinas's point is that virtual particles popping out of empty space is exactly what you would expect if God really exists, because then there couldn't be such a thing as true nothingness: there would still be God.

4. The Argument from Degree

In his fourth argument, Aquinas focuses on differences in degree that are found in the world. Things can be hot or cold, good or bad. He says that in order for there to be a comparison of good and bad, then there must be something against which we are comparing them. Hence, there must be ultimate goodness or justice. That pinnacle of all things we call God.

C. S. Lewis held to this when he began to reject atheism. In his book *Mere Christianity*, he writes "My argument against God was that the universe seemed so cruel and unjust. But how had I got this idea of just and unjust? A man does not call a line crooked unless he has some idea of a straight line.... Of course I could have given up my idea of justice by saying it was nothing but a private idea of my own. But if I did that, then my argument against God collapsed too."[5] If there is such a thing as evil and goodness, then there must be something to which we compare all things. According to Aquinas and Lewis, we call that God.

5. The Teleological Argument

Aquinas's fifth argument is often called the watchmaker analogy, because by looking at a watch you understand that someone designed the watch. Since there is a purpose to the object, there must be an intelligent designer who created the watch. If an object has a design, then there is a designer. The reason this is called the teleological argument is that the Greek word *telos* means purpose or end (goal). The moon and the stars and humanity appear designed, and they operate according to basic laws, hence there must be a designer or lawmaker, and we call that person God.

Of Aquinas's five arguments, the teleological argument has come to be recognized as the weakest. Scientists have come to understand how complexity that appears to be designed can be the result of millions of years of evolution. Our eyes, for instance, are of amazingly complex design, and yet evolutionary history provides a plausible account of how they developed without being designed.

This weakness of this argument is precisely why we shouldn't take any of the five arguments by themselves but rather as connected. Together they support the theist belief that there must be some being we call God that is the cause of the world's existence, holding it in motion, serving as the model for love and justice and perfection, leading creation to some grand purpose or end (*telos*). Individual portions of these arguments can be disputed, but their beauty lies in the way they function together to create a compelling whole. The fact that we exist and ask questions leads us back to the cause and designer of it all, the entity that we call God.

The Ontological Argument

Another style of proof was developed by a great church theologian two centuries before Aquinas: Saint Anselm, the eleventh-century Archbishop of Canterbury. His proof is called the ontological argument, because it deals with the very nature of being; the proof derives from the very essence of who God is. Anselm developed the argument in his work *The Proslogion* and concluded: "Therefore there is absolutely no doubt that something-than-which-a-greater-cannot-be-thought exists both in the mind and the reality." Let's walk through his logic.

We start with the nature of God. God is "something-than-which-a-greater-cannot-be-thought." That part is simple to understand—that God is, by definition, the greatest possible being. We can imagine this being and think about this being in our mind. We do this all the time, when we pray to God and worship him. Every time we claim that God is good and holy, we are giving him attributes of the greatest thing possible.

Anselm's argument is that if God doesn't exist, then it creates within us a contradiction. We can imagine God, but if that being is just a figment of our imagination, then we have done the impossible: imagined something greater than the greatest thing. There can be nothing greater than the greatest thing, so God must exist both in reality and in the mind. This is the core of Anselm's ontological argument.

The standard objection to Anselm was made by a contemporary of his, Guanillo, who posited that just because you can imagine something doesn't mean it has to exist. Guanillo proposed the idea of a perfect island—you can imagine such a thing, but that doesn't mean it exists. However, one could counter that Guanillo's objection illustrates a misunderstanding of how fundamentally different God is from all other entities. What makes an island perfect? Is it the temperature? The quality of sand on the beach? There is an almost infinite number of descriptors that might vary from one person to another. Charles Hartshorne, a twentieth-century philosopher, counters in this way: "[An] 'unsurpassable, necessary island' is nonsense," but God is, by definition "entirely necessary, as well as unsurpassable."[6] Anslem's argument works precisely because God is not a random dirt pile rising out of the sea, but the necessary entity that is greater than all things.

That same philosopher, Charles Hartshorne, has pushed Anselm's thought further, making it both clearer and more helpful for our age. God is by nature fundamentally different from every other entity. We speak of God as perfect, which makes God unique and (because we can conceive of such perfection) necessarily something that exists. But the perfection of God makes God even more unique, because "the term 'perfect' (not conceivably surpassable by another) is as abstract as the term 'imperfect'; but whereas there are innumerable possible kinds of imperfect individuals, there can be but one perfect individual."[7] This individual is God and is related to Aquinas's argument of degree. Hartshorne's version of the ontological argument brought C. S. Lewis to faith—that is, the very nature of the fact that we can imagine something as perfect (whether perfect in terms of love or justice) means there must be some basis for it in reality.

This proof and Aquinas's arguments do not provide definitive evidence for God, but together they demonstrate that theism is rational and logically consistent. Atheists, on the other hand, believe that nothing caused or sustains the universe and believe that our common ideas of love, justice, and perfection are mere figments of happenstance and chance.

Pascal's Wager

If the proofs are not definitive, how are we to choose? Often people defer to Pascal's Wager, which is not a proof but addresses the agnostic worldview. Essentially it boils down to this: What happens if each side is wrong? If atheism is wrong, then there is no downside; but if theists are wrong, then the downside is not merely being plunged into hell but missing out on paradise. Therefore, why not choose the one that has the least downside? This argument is like going to Las Vegas and being allowed to keep the money if you win but not having to pay if you lose. Under those circumstances, having nothing to lose, who wouldn't make a bet?

Pascal's Wager may be the most logical of the options: a mild agnosticism that leads to nominal faith, on the off chance that God exists. But a decision to follow this plan is not what we would call wisdom. Faith is about more than being right; it is about hope, and hope, ultimately, is about wisdom.

Wisdom and Faith

We know a young woman who graduated from seminary and had learned all the proofs for God. She knew Scripture and had grown up in church, yet at some point she had lost her faith. She sat, crying, and said, "How do I believe in God again? I just can't escape the idea that this world is hopeless." She was desperate to believe again, because without God the world seemed to be just a random collection of atoms and molecules that somehow happened to have formed her. Without God there was no future after death, no past before birth, and no meaning to being human. Love was stripped down to chemical reactions in the brain, and self-sacrifice was reduced to evolutionary principles of protecting offspring. How would she gain wisdom? How could she believe in God again?

She knew the answer was not in offering more or better proofs of God. The proofs we have are enough to demonstrate that faith in God can be rational, but faith and wisdom are about more than proof. One reason we know that is because Scripture, which contains all things necessary for salvation, does not attempt to prove God. Scripture simply presumes that there is one. Scripture has arguments for Jesus being raised from the dead and therefore Jesus being God, but not for the existence of God. It presumes that wisdom includes a faith in God and describes the opposite of wisdom in this way: "Fools say in their hearts, There is no God" (Psalm 14:1).

Wisdom, then, is living as if there is a God even if you do not yet believe. This is not the same as Pascal's Wager, which is deciding on a nominal faith just in case there is a God. Rather, wisdom is living every day so as to put yourself into a position where you can live with hope. John Wesley, the founder of Methodism, once experienced despair very much like the young woman in our story. He, too, had been to seminary, knew the Scriptures and the arguments for God, and yet he had lost hope and faith. He was then given this advice: "Preach faith until you have faith." He tried it, and after a time he heard the message of faith again, had a changed heart, and once again was able to live a life of faith and hope. Rather than accepting agnosticism, he chose to live as if hope was real—and then discovered that it was.

This world is so full of love and hope that it must have a source beyond ourselves, and we call that source God. People often ask us how to convince their children or parents or friends to believe in God. It isn't by sitting them down and walking through proofs; it is by living a compelling life of hope. At some point in everyone's life, atheism and agnosticism are going to prove insufficient. The question will change from "How can I believe in a God I can't prove?" to "How can I afford not to believe in God when faith, life, and hope are offered?"

This is what Jesus embodied when he was on this earth. He did not present logical proofs to his disciples, but rather ate with tax collectors, healed lepers, and created a community of love and hope that was built on Christ himself. This is who we call God.

Rapid Response

Your non-Christian friend says, "Okay, I don't want a long, complicated answer, but tell me this: "How can you trust God when you can't prove that God even exists? You can't see God or touch God, so how can you believe in God?"

You might say, "Proof about God goes both ways. We can't prove that God doesn't exist just as we can't prove that God does exist. In fact, the only proof we have is that we exist and that we have life and hope. I'm not interested in proving God; I want to live the life that a great and perfect God made possible."

5.
Can I Trust the
Old Testament?

5.
Can I Trust the Old Testament?

The Old Testament is really, really old. It describes not only the beginning of the universe, but events that may have occurred three thousand years ago. Scholars believe it was composed in a variety of ways, taking its final form about a hundred years before Christ, so even as a body of literature it is at least two thousand years old. Many parts of it are centuries older than that. It was written by a people who lived in an obscure part of the world, the Middle East, and who were not the most powerful or culturally influential group of their time.

It was written in Hebrew and Aramaic and contains many different kinds of literature. Genesis has stories that ancient people told to explain the history of the world. Deuteronomy has laws governing what today we would describe as moral, political, and religious matters. Psalms has poetry that has been and continues to be used in worship and personal devotions. Proverbs has short sayings of wisdom about how best to live one's life. Isaiah has prophetic pronouncements describing the people's situation at that time and looking to the future. Daniel has both historical narrative and visions of the future that are often called apocalyptic.

Christians disagree about exactly what constitutes the Old Testament. Roman Catholics and Eastern Orthodox used a version that was written in Greek called the Septuagint. That version was translated into Latin and for 1,500 years was the Old Testament for the two largest branches of Christianity. During the Reformation, Protestants discovered that Jews used a different

Bible, one with fewer books. In their attempt to reform the church, Protestants started using only those books recognized by the Jews, and the remaining materials were grouped by Protestants into a collection of texts outside the Old Testament called the Apocrypha. These texts are still included in the Bible used by Catholics and Orthodox.

This discrepancy in the number of books in the Old Testament arose because of the way it was written and how it became Holy Scripture for the Jewish people. The Jews regard their Bible (what Christians call the Old Testament) as having three parts. The first two parts—the Law and the Prophets—were seen as Scripture during Jesus' lifetime. In the Sermon on the Mount, Jesus taught the Golden Rule as a summary of Scripture by referring to the two parts: "Therefore, you should treat people in the same way that you want people to treat you; this is the Law and the Prophets" (Matthew 7:12). The Law included the first five books of our Old Testament: Genesis, Exodus, Leviticus, Numbers, and Deuteronomy. The Prophets included Joshua, Judges, 1 and 2 Samuel, 1 and 2 Kings, Isaiah, Jeremiah, Lamentations, Ezekiel, and the twelve Minor Prophets. Jews grouped the rest of our Old Testament books into a third section called the Writings, which included Psalms and Proverbs. Because the list of books accepted into this third group was still being decided when Christianity began, there are different versions of Scripture. Protestant Christians follow the consensus that was adopted by Jewish leaders, and Roman Catholic and Orthodox Christians follow what the first-century Christians used as their Bible.

Because it was written so long ago in a cultural context very different from ours, people outside the Christian faith ask hard questions about the content of the Old Testament. One such critic is Richard Dawkins, a scientist who has written in favor of atheism. He put it very bluntly when he wrote,

> The God of the Old Testament is arguably the most unpleasant character in all fiction: jealous and proud of it; a petty, unjust, unforgiving control-freak; a vindictive, bloodthirsty ethnic cleanser; a misogynistic, homophobic, racist, infanticidal, genocidal, filicidal, pestilential, megalomaniacal, sadomasochistic, capriciously malevolent bully.[1]

One does not have to agree with Dawkins's views to acknowledge that there are difficult passages in the Old Testament. Though his summary is a one-sided, exaggerated characterization, it is true that in many places the God portrayed in the Old Testament is described as saying and doing things about which Christians today are embarrassed.

Many faithful Christians wonder if they can believe that the Old Testament is truly inspired. They ask, "Can I trust this ancient document? Does it really reveal important truths about God and humanity and how we should live today?"

Christians today believe that the Old Testament is part of God's self-revelation to his chosen people. God made a covenant with Abraham, promising to make Abraham's descendants a chosen people with their own land if they would worship God and follow God's laws. God's relationship with Isaac, Jacob, and their descendants developed over time. Stories were told, and the commandments of God were passed down. Eventually, the oral traditions were written into the books we have today. The Old Testament is our written record of how Abraham's descendants heard the word of God in their time.

To summarize our perspective, Christians believe that the Old Testament is the foundation of the New Testament, but that some of its key teachings have been changed by the life, death, and resurrection of Jesus.

The Old Testament as Foundation of the New Testament

All Christians agree that the Old Testament is the foundation of the New Testament and carries authority for Christians today. There are more than 250 citations of Old Testament texts in the New Testament writings, and if allusions are counted, that number goes even higher. For the creators of the New Testament, the Old Testament was their Scripture and was an authority to be cited, interpreted, and referred to. It provided the basis to understand what God had done in the life, death, and resurrection of Jesus. The Christian movement was a continuation of what God had done before as recounted in the Old Testament.

The Old Testament foundation is especially evident in the Gospel of Matthew. In the first two chapters, Matthew recounts the ancestors of Jesus (drawn from Old Testament sources) and then quotes Isaiah, Hosea, Micah, and Jeremiah. Matthew's understanding of Jesus' birth and identity is deeply tied to his understanding of the Old Testament and its meaning for his day. Matthew's account makes this relationship with the Old Testament especially clear:

> Six days later Jesus took Peter, James, and John his brother, and brought them to the top of a very high mountain. He was transformed in front of them. His face shone like the sun, and his clothes became as white as light. Moses and Elijah appeared to them, talking with Jesus. Peter reacted to all of this by saying to Jesus, "Lord, it's good that we're here. If you want, I'll make three shrines: one for you, one for Moses, and one for Elijah." While he was still speaking, look, a bright cloud overshadowed them. A voice from the cloud said, "This is my Son whom I dearly love. I am very pleased with him. Listen to him!" (Matthew 17:1-5)

The experience of Peter, James, and John on the Mount of Transfiguration had two key points. First, as with the baptism of Jesus, God spoke to make it clear that Jesus was the Son of God. The disciples were learning that he was not simply another rabbi or even a new prophet—he was the Messiah. Second, the vision of Jesus talking with Moses and Elijah was very symbolic. Though God was doing a new thing in Jesus, it was done in continuity with all that had gone before. Moses represented the Law; Elijah represented the Prophets. The mountaintop encounter showed that Jesus' ministry was building on and fulfilling what had been said and done in the Jewish Scripture.

Jesus himself made a similar point. In the Sermon on the Mount, he said,

> "Don't even begin to think that I have come to do away with the Law and the Prophets. I haven't come to do away with them but to fulfill them. I say to you very seriously that as long as heaven and earth exist, neither the smallest letter nor even the smallest stroke of a pen will be erased from the Law

until everything there becomes a reality. Therefore, whoever ignores one of the least of these commands and teaches others to do the same will be called the lowest in the kingdom of heaven. But whoever keeps these commands and teaches people to keep them will be called great in the kingdom of heaven. I say to you that unless your righteousness is greater than the righteousness of the legal experts and the Pharisees, you will never enter the kingdom of heaven." (Matthew 5:17-20)

Jesus then proceeded to interpret certain Old Testament passages by strengthening the expectations contained in them. The condemnation of adultery was affirmed, but Jesus taught that lust is also wrong. He said that murder violates the law, but so does anger.

Jesus' Interpretation of Old Testament Laws

The religious leaders of Jesus' day were having significant conversations about how to interpret the many Old Testament laws. By one count, people believed there were 613 different commandments. The Pharisees were a group of Jewish scholars who believed that obedience to these commandments was the most important way of serving God.

While not repudiating any of the laws directly, Jesus interpreted the laws using his own approach. He thus entered into the theological conversations of his day, angering some of the scribes and Pharisees because he taught with authority—as if he knew the answer. He was willing to have conversations with women and tax collectors. He ate dinner with those deemed to be sinners. Some religious leaders were so focused on ritual purity and holiness that they tended to exclude persons deemed undesirable or in violation of the law; Jesus, in contrast, tended to interpret the Old Testament with a focus on broadening the community. He tended to cross boundaries and reach out to those who had been excluded.

The religious scholars of Jesus' time were also debating how many laws should be seen in relation to each other. Though the scholars believed that all the laws should be obeyed, there was a sense that some laws were more important than others. Jesus' interpretation of the Old Testament was expressed in his criticism of these scholars, when he said they were paying attention to minor points of the law rather than the most important parts. He told them,

> "How terrible it will be for you legal experts and Pharisees! Hypocrites! You give to God a tenth of mint, dill, and cumin, but you forget about the more important matters of the Law: justice, peace, and faith. You ought to give a tenth but without forgetting about those more important matters. You blind guides! You filter out an ant but swallow a camel. How terrible it will be for you legal experts and Pharisees! Hypocrites! You clean the outside of the cup and plate, but inside they are full of violence and pleasure seeking. Blind Pharisee! First clean the inside of the cup so that the outside of the cup will be clean too." (Matthew 23:23-26)

Jesus' words in this passage are consistent with his overall approach of affirming the Old Testament while reorienting the people of his day toward its most important message. In this way he was very much like the Old Testament prophets, who continually said that some of the commandments were more important than others.

The question of the laws' relative importance arose explicitly when Jesus was asked one of the most difficult biblical questions of his time. A lawyer asked him, "Teacher, which commandment in the law is the greatest?" Jesus answered by citing Deuteronomy 6:5 and Leviticus 19:18.

> He replied, "You must love the Lord your God with all your heart, with all your being, and with all your mind. This is the first and greatest commandment. And the second is like it: You must love your neighbor as you love yourself. All the Law and the Prophets depend on these two commands."
> (Matthew 22:37-40)

In his answer, Jesus not only named the most important commandments. He claimed that all the rest of Jewish Scripture hangs on them. When you think about the number and complexity of the Old Testament books and all the different types of literature they contain—let alone several hundred commandments—Jesus' claim was astounding: that the fundamental and organizing principle of the Old Testament is love of God and love of neighbor as of self.

The Old Testament and the Gentiles

After Jesus' death and resurrection, the apostles were faced with a very difficult problem. An important part of the Jewish way of life was following dietary laws. Jews were not allowed to eat pork, shellfish, or food sacrificed to idols, and they were not to have table fellowship with Gentiles. In addition to the dietary laws, males were to be circumcised.

The Book of Acts recounts how Christianity began to be embraced by Gentiles, especially those who were called "God-fearers." These Gentiles often participated in Jewish worship but would not convert to Judaism, in part because of the strict rules. When some Gentiles received the gifts of the Holy Spirit, and after Peter had a vision from God about including Gentiles in the Christian community, a full-blown crisis faced the community. Did Gentiles who committed their lives to Jesus as Lord and Savior have to be circumcised and follow the Old Testament commandments about food?

There were many opinions on this matter, and finally a council was held in Jerusalem as recounted in Acts 15. During that conference, reports were given about the amazing things God had done among the Gentiles and how the Holy Spirit had been given to them. Passages from Scripture were cited about how Gentiles could find the Lord. In response, the council concluded by sending a letter to Christians everywhere that said,

> The Holy Spirit has led us to the decision that no burden should be placed on you other than these essentials: refuse food offered to idols, blood, the meat from strangled animals, and sexual immorality. You will do well to avoid such things. Farewell. (Acts 15:28-29)

In essence, Gentiles who accepted Jesus as Lord and Savior and were baptized into the church were required to follow moral laws, but they didn't have to follow the Jewish dietary commandments or be circumcised.

Difficult Passages in the Old Testament

The Old Testament is the foundation for the new covenant Jesus inaugurated, but there are still major problems in relating the two. The Old Testament has some very difficult passages that seem to describe a very different religion and different God from the one described in the New Testament. There are many such passages, but let us consider them in three categories.

Some passages portray a God who instructs Israel to wage war against its enemies in vicious and extreme ways. The battle account in the Book of Joshua often portray God requiring Israel to kill all the inhabitants of a city—men, women, children, and animals. God commanded the Israelites to do so to the people of Jericho (except for their spy Rahab and her family) and then also to the people of Ai. God required the Israelites to burn cities on several occasions and to destroy property. Throughout the books of the Old Testament, war is portrayed as a normal way of life, and God is seen as taking the side of Israel against its enemies.

This portrayal of God seems contradictory to the vision put forth by the Old Testament prophets who foresaw a time when "God will judge between the nations, and settle disputes of mighty nations. Then they will beat their swords into iron plows and their spears into pruning tools. Nation will not take up sword against nation; they will no longer learn how to make war" (Isaiah 2:4).

In addition to waging war, God is portrayed in the Old Testament as violently punishing people in unjust ways. In 1 Kings 18, Elijah confronts the prophets of a rival God, Baal, and challenges them to a contest. Elijah's God proves victorious, and immediately afterward Elijah instructs the people to kill all the prophets of Baal.

Slavery is fact of life throughout the Old Testament, and God is seen as giving instructions for how slaves are to be treated. On Mount Sinai, for example, God tells Moses,

Regarding male or female slaves that you are allowed to have: You can buy a male or a female slave from the nations that are around you. You can also buy them from the foreign guests who live with you and from their extended families that are with you, who were born in your land. These can belong to you as property. You can pass them on to your children as inheritance that they can own as permanent property. You can make these people work as slaves, but you must not rule harshly over your own people, the Israelites.

(Leviticus 25:44-46)

Such passages were used by Christians prior to the American Civil War to justify the practice of slavery.

Many of the disagreements between modern science and Christianity are based on Old Testament passages. As mentioned previously, Archbishop James Ussher, a seventeenth-century primate of the Church of Ireland, took the chronology of Genesis very literally, calculating that the world was created October 23, 4004 B.C. Charles Darwin and other nineteenth-century scientists, looking at physical evidence and making assumptions about evolutionary and geological changes, began to postulate a much earlier date for creation. Scientists now estimate that the so-called big bang of creation occurred almost fourteen billion years ago. On the surface, this appears to contradict the six-day creation story in Genesis 1.

There are other scientific problems as well. The story of the flood in Genesis 6–9 presumes a three-tiered universe with waters above the dome and waters under the earth. That view was the best science in 1000 B.C., but it no longer fits the knowledge we have. When Joshua asked the Lord to make the sun stand still during the battle against the Amorites, God did so. Of course, such an account is contrary to everything that modern science tells us about the universe.

Passages such as these—depicting a God of war, violence, slavery, and scientific absurdities—are reasons why so many readers are reluctant to trust the Old Testament.

Modern Interpretation of the Old Testament

All Christians believe that the Old Testament is the inspired word of God. Some believe it is inerrant—without mistakes of any kind. Most Christians have a different perspective on it. They see the Bible as authoritative in matters of faith and practice, containing what human beings need to know for salvation, but they believe inspiration does not mean infallibility. It does mean that God gave the human authors a message that should be conveyed to God's people. By reading the text, we connect with God and God's purposes for humankind.

The Old Testament documents were originally written for people who lived in ancient times. They came at a time when people had limited knowledge of the larger world in which they lived. Most Christians acknowledge that God was using human beings as conduits for God's message, and that their specific cultural realities shaped the text, including their views on science, violence, and war.

In terms of science, Bible scholars for centuries have taught that God accommodated himself to the capacities of his human audience. God is beyond human comprehension today, and that was also true in ancient times. What if God had tried to explain to the ancient Hebrews the big bang theory, the process of evolution, and the age of the universe? Instead, his message was both beautiful and understandable to God's audience: "In the beginning, God created the heavens and the earth" (Genesis 1:1 NIV).

With regard to violence, God's revelation has to be seen in the context of two important factors. First, the ancient Middle East was an incredibly violent place. War was the norm, and punishment by death was a frequent penalty for crime. Fighting often escalated, and a small matter could ignite war between tribes or nations. In that context, enunciating the punishment of "an eye for an eye, a tooth for a tooth, a hand for a hand, a foot for a foot" (Exodus 21:24) actually limited the amount of violence that would be permitted.

Second, Israel was a small nation in the midst of many other hostile peoples. God was understood to be guiding them into a new land. Conquest was part of the normal give-and-take among peoples of that time, and God was siding with the Israelites in order to accomplish God's larger purposes.

Over time, God was able to reveal more and more of God's rule of love into human hearts. The prophets announced the vision of swords being beaten into iron plows, and Jesus reinforced that vision with his teaching about the kingdom of God. The New Covenant does fulfill and complete what was begun in the Old Covenant; yet the people of Israel, today's Jewish people, still have a role to play in God's plan to save the world.

Jesus reoriented the apostles toward a different approach to the Old Testament as seen in the examples discussed above. Christians since the first century have come to understand that parts of the Old Testament are still binding on Christians, and parts are not. Many churches teach that there are three types of commandments in the Old Testament: civil, ceremonial, and moral.

Civil commandments dealt with crime and punishment and the organization of society among the Hebrew people. Many of their rules seem severe today, such as punishments of death for being disobedient to one's parents. Other civil laws, such as using honest weights and measures in business transactions, are still seen as helpful today.

Other commandments were ceremonial, governing how God was to be worshiped. Jews practiced animal sacrifice, and there were regulations for what kinds of animals should be offered on what occasions and how the offering was to be used. The leadership of worship was invested in priests and Levites, and the rules governing their selection and behavior were included in the law. Such practices governed Hebrew worship for centuries. Animal sacrifices were still being offered at the Temple in Jerusalem during Jesus' lifetime. For Christians, though, Christ's death on the cross was seen to be the ultimate sacrifice for the sins of the world. For that reason, Gentile Christians were not bound by the sacrificial commandments of the former covenant. For Jewish Christians, the destruction of the Temple in A.D. 70 brought the sacrificial practices to an end as well.

Other laws were deemed to be moral laws. Chief among these for Christians are the Ten Commandments, found in Exodus 20:2-17. Such laws dealt with key behaviors for individuals. Other moral laws dealt with how the Jews were to treat widows, orphans, and aliens living among them.

After the apostolic conference described in Acts 15, the moral commandments were seen as binding on Christians, but the civil and ceremonial commandments were not binding. They were part of the old covenant. Christ had instituted a new covenant

In spite of the council's ruling, Christians have struggled for centuries with how the Old Testament is to be interpreted. On the one hand, the God whom Jesus called Father is the same God as the one who called Abraham and spoke through Moses and the prophets. Jesus taught that his ministry was a fulfillment of the promises made and the commandments taught in the Scriptures of his time. On the other hand, it is clear that in Jesus, God was doing something new.

As a result, Christians have retained the Bible that Jesus used and called it the Old Covenant. The new relationship to God that Christ taught, based as it was on what God had done before, was called the New Covenant. The Greek word for *covenant* was later translated as "testament," and the names for the two parts of the Christian Bible—Old Testament and New Testament—became common usage in English.

The best way to interpret the Old Testament, then, is never to pick out a single verse and assume it is the ultimate word. Instead, we should understand that each verse is to be interpreted as part of the whole Bible's message. When there are confusing or apparently immoral verses in Scripture, we should always test them against the message of Christ and the New Testament.

Rapid Response

Imagine that you are in a coffee shop hanging out, and suddenly your non-Christian friend says, "Okay, I don't want a long complicated answer, but tell me this: Why should I believe that a collection of books this old, with this many confusing and difficult passages, should have any importance in my life today?"

You might say, "It's all about how you interpret the Old Testament. God spoke to people long ago in ways they could understand. Yes, there are lots of things that made sense three thousand years ago and we don't believe today. But there are also important truths contained in those books that we really need to hear. The important part is reading the whole Bible to get the message of the entire book."

6.
Are Marriage, Sex, and Family Life Religious Issues?

6.
Are Marriage, Sex, and Family Life Religious Issues?

Sex is controversial. It is the most private of acts, and yet it is very public in movies, courts, churches, billboards, and our schools. Courts and churches and the public in general differ on beliefs about sexuality. Some avoid the conversation, while others speak boldly and even protest based on their beliefs about sexuality.

What is the right approach? Is sex public or private? Should churches have a public stance on sexuality? Should sex even be a religious issue at all? Does God really care what we do in our bedrooms?

Whether or not God cares about our sex lives, churches most definitely do. One church in Dallas gained publicity for a sermon series and a book when the pastor slept with his wife for twenty-four hours in a king-size bed on the roof of his church. When Arthur was a freshman at the University of Kansas, he belonged to a prominent college ministry that considered sexual purity one of the key elements of a Christian life. One of the leaders of that ministry took the promise so seriously that he and his wife did not even kiss until their wedding day. Though most Christians are not that restrictive, many take a pledge of some kind. Arthur's wife, Becky, was part of a church in high school that asked youth to sign a pledge restricting sexual activity in a program called True Love Waits. This was the pledge:

Believing that true love waits, I make a commitment to God, myself, my family, my friends, my future mate, and my future children to be sexually abstinent from this day until the day I enter a biblical marriage relationship.

The public perception about churches and sexuality is that religion exists to restrict sexual activity. This becomes very clear if you live in Topeka, Kansas. It's the home of Westboro Baptist Church, a small, family-based congregation that is driven by an anti-gay agenda. They own websites stating that God hates people of alternate sexual orientations, and they spend time protesting every event that could possibly be associated with homosexuality. They picket churches, community groups, and the University of Kansas. They are especially infamous for picketing funerals of military servicemen and women. This church is on the fringes of Christianity, but the impression left on young people is that, no matter what a person's sexual orientation is, the religious community's approach to sex is generally: Don't do it!

Such religious restrictions on sex seem antiquated today. At one point in the 1950s it was too scandalous for Ricky and Lucy, a married couple, to sleep in the same bed on the TV show *I Love Lucy*. Today television shows regularly show sexual scenes and couples clad in their underwear. In 1997, the movie *Titanic* made waves when it showed a sex scene with nudity, even though the film was rated PG-13, which seemed to be saying that our culture accepts nudity and sex as appropriate for thirteen-year-olds. In the forty-seven years between Lucy and *Titanic*, things certainly did change! And they have kept changing. In 2014, a major pornographic website called Pornhub advertised in Times Square. Protests took the ad down after forty-eight hours, but the fact that such an advertisement was allowed there in the first place demonstrates how dramatically things have changed.

Religious groups, though perceived as being behind the times, are not immune from the sexual revolution. Christian Mingle and J-Date (a Jewish dating site equivalent to Christian Mingle) joined together in 2013 for a dating survey and asked, "Would you have sex before marriage?" Eighty-six percent of the respondents said yes.

From our personal experience as pastors, we know that this is normal. Many young people who seek to get married in church and live a Christian life come to premarital counseling living with their significant other. They are nervous to sit in a pastor's office and admit they have been having sex for years, but it is frequently the case. It isn't that their faith is irrelevant, but rather that the restrictions on sex seem irrelevant. In a survey taken the following year, Christian Mingle and J-Date asked whether or not respondents were interested in marrying someone of the same faith, and 68 percent of all persons (not just religious persons) said yes. This combination of valuing religious traditions and ignoring sexual traditions prompted a new phrase: "sexual atheists."

Fundamentally, our culture seems to have decided that whether or not God exists, we don't want religion imposing on our sex life. This new phenomenon raises some interesting questions: Does God really care about my sex life? Are churches missing the point, or has our culture strayed? Does Scripture detail any goals or values regarding sex?

Scripture and Sex

Scripture is the story of God's interactions with the world, offering us salvation and the hope of living a full life. But what defines a full life? Is it family? Food? Sex? From the first chapter in Scripture when God creates humanity and gives instructions to "be fertile and multiply; fill the earth" (Genesis 1:28), sex has had some part in God's plans for us. It's amusing to think that this first guideline about sex in Scripture is the exact opposite of what young people might expect. Instead of Don't do it! God says, Do it! From the first pages of the Bible, sex is meant to be something good—part of the full life that God has for us.

But we tend to abuse good gifts. Sex was designed to be a positive force in our lives, but in our world it has become a form of oppression, a source of regret, and a place of brokenness. People are haunted by sexual pasts they are ashamed of. Marriages are ripped apart by affairs, youth are obsessed by pornography, and lust dominates the media. If sex is positive, why is it the source of so much pain? Sex is not the primary topic of Scripture, but it mirrors the basic story of Scripture: we are good but full of brokenness.

Scripture tells us that the misuse of sex is not new but a problem of every generation. The Book of Ecclesiastes puts it this way: "Whatever has happened—that's what will happen again; whatever has occurred—that's what will occur again. There's nothing new under the sun" (Ecclesiastes 1:9). Our repeated sexual issues are the cause of quite a few Scriptures about sex in the Old Testament. The Book of Leviticus, for example, has an entire chapter on sex, mostly consisting of basic restrictions that we would endorse today, such as don't have sex with your mother (Leviticus 18:7) and don't have sex with your sister (Leviticus 18:9). Other Old Testament passages have sexual themes, such as Proverbs 6:32, which says "He who commits adultery is senseless. Doing so, he destroys himself." Whether or not we agree with all the rules in the Old Testament, the original intent was to help the Israelites live sexual lives that were less broken.

When Jesus entered the picture, he did not address most sexual issues. Jesus was never once recorded speaking about homosexuality, for example, or even obvious restrictions such as incest. Sometimes, noting his lack of comments about sex, people are led to believe or hope that Jesus was as apathetic about the Old Testament sexual restrictions as we are. This is not so. In fact, Jesus may have been even stricter about some sexual matters. In the Sermon on the Mount, Jesus taught, "You have heard that it was said, *Don't commit adultery.* But I say to you that every man who looks at a woman lustfully has already committed adultery in his heart" (Matthew 5:27-28). If Jesus' teaching is true, then every person has committed adultery of some sort. Jesus was increasing the need for sexual purity, rather than removing it or being apathetic about it. Why, then, do some people think he didn't care about sex? Why would we follow Jesus when he seems to have unrealistic standards about our sex life? It's because Jesus wants something better for us.

Many times, Jesus encountered people who did not live up to the high standards of Scripture, and every time Jesus provided grace. Once, Jesus met a woman at a well—a Samaritan he was not even supposed to speak with—and she had a troubled past.

> Jesus said to her, "Go, get your husband, and come back here."
> The woman replied, "I don't have a husband." "You are right

to say, 'I don't have a husband,'" Jesus answered. "You've had five husbands, and the man that you are with now isn't your husband. You've spoken the truth." The woman said, "Sir, I see that you are a prophet." (John 4:16-19)

Jesus did not condemn the woman. Instead he offered her grace and hope. Jesus made her the evangelist to her community as she ran to tell everyone that she had met Jesus.

A similar situation occurred when Jesus was having dinner with a Pharisee named Simon. A woman with a troubled sexual past walked in, washed Jesus' feet with her tears, and poured perfumed oil on them. Her actions upset the Pharisee, who understood the high sexual standards that God has for his people. The Pharisee judged both the woman and Jesus.

> Jesus turned to the woman and said to Simon, "Do you see this woman? When I entered your home, you didn't give me water for my feet, but she wet my feet with tears and wiped them with her hair. You didn't greet me with a kiss, but she hasn't stopped kissing my feet since I came in. You didn't anoint my head with oil, but she has poured perfumed oil on my feet. This is why I tell you that her many sins have been forgiven; so she has shown great love. The one who is forgiven little loves little." (Luke 7:44-47)

The Pharisee was ready to condemn the woman because of the scriptural rules about sex, but once again Jesus showed grace and mercy. She was forgiven without a single word of judgment.

One final story, found in John 8, will help clarify the nature of Jesus and sexual restrictions. This passage is well known, but you might notice that this section of John is marked in some Bibles because this particular story does not appear in the earliest manuscripts, meaning that it's quite possible this story never actually happened. We use it here not to make a statement about its authenticity, but rather because it so accurately summarizes the type of person Jesus was and helps us understand why Jesus has high expectations for those who follow him and yet unconditional grace for those who fall.

The legal experts and Pharisees brought a woman caught in adultery. Placing her in the center of the group, they said to Jesus, "Teacher, this woman was caught in the act of committing adultery. In the Law, Moses commanded us to stone women like this. What do you say?" They said this to test him, because they wanted a reason to bring an accusation against him. Jesus bent down and wrote on the ground with his finger. They continued to question him, so he stood up and replied, "Whoever hasn't sinned should throw the first stone." Bending down again, he wrote on the ground. Those who heard him went away, one by one, beginning with the elders. Finally, only Jesus and the woman were left in the middle of the crowd. Jesus stood up and said to her, "Woman, where are they? Is there no one to condemn you?" She said, "No one, sir." Jesus said, "Neither do I condemn you. Go, and from now on, don't sin anymore." (John 8:3-11)

This story is significant because it sounds like the same Jesus who offered grace to the woman at the well and to the prostitute who washed Jesus' feet with her hair, and yet it clarifies the challenge of keeping up sexual purity laws. The legal experts and Pharisees sound similar to the rigid, seemingly anti-sex religious leaders of today, and Jesus found himself faced with a decision—either to support the law or the broken person in front of him. If he supported the law, then he would be allowing a woman to be stoned to death, and yet if he supported the woman he would be violating the law that he himself believed in. Jesus found a different way, maintaining the goal of sexual purity while at the same time extending grace to the sinner.

Jesus did not come to abolish restrictions about adultery; in fact, he increased them. Not every person has committed adultery, but all of us have looked at someone else with lust in our heart. By Jesus' reckoning, every human is a sinner, and therefore no one has a right to judge. The views on sexual purity held by legal scholars and Pharisees were not too high; they were too low. If the scholars had possessed Jesus' wisdom, they would have known that they, like the woman, had sinned. Thus, when Jesus looked at the woman and the rigid religious leaders, he had compassion for all of them.

The key to that passage is in the final line, which sums up Jesus' approach to sexual issues throughout his ministry. After the judgmental religious people had left, Jesus saw that no one had thrown a stone to condemn the woman, and he said, "Neither do I condemn you. Go, and from now on, don't sin anymore."

Jesus has high expectations and high grace. He knows we are going to fail in our sexual lives, and he provides constant forgiveness so that we might go and live a better sexual life, one that might provide a path to a full life.

When we fall short, we need both the high expectations and high grace. The tension between these two seemingly different standards was lived out in the lives of two men who became friends and youth leaders at church. We will call them Ted and Jim.

As a teaching lesson for the youth one evening, Ted told them the following story: One day he got a call to meet his wife at the doctor's office. As soon as he walked in, Ted knew something was wrong. Evidently, his wife had just tested positive for HIV. She said she had never cheated on him, so the doctor turned to Ted and asked him to confess the affair or affairs that had caused him to contract and transmit HIV. Ted was shocked. He had never cheated, but how else could he explain the positive test? He told the doctor, "Run the test again." The doctor rolled his eyes, saying that everyone denies it and that he had never seen a false positive. "Just tell us," said the doctor. Ted looked the doctor in the eye and said "It isn't me. Run the test again." Sure enough, it was an extraordinarily rare false positive. Ted was vindicated.

That's where Jim took over. He told the youth that his story was different. If he had been in Ted's position, he would not have been able to look the doctor in the eye, because the story of his earlier life was one of sin and brokenness. He said, "I have scars from my past that I wish I could remove. God has taken my brokenness and offered me grace and turned my scars into something beautiful. I don't want you to have the same scars. I'm telling you this so you will live your life differently. I hope you'll be able to tell the doctor, 'Run the test again.' I can't change my past, but maybe I can help you change your future."

Jesus sets high expectations, offering us a path that will lead to a full life. But he also provides high grace, so that when they fall, as Jim did, we can experience redemption from a broken past and the possibility of a full life in the future.

When Scripture Says Yes: Sex in the Christian Life

In a culture that expects the church to say no to sex, let's flip the tables. Where does Scripture encourage sex? What about when Scripture says yes?

To begin, let's return to the beginning of Genesis, when God created the first man and woman and said, "This is the reason that a man leaves his father and mother and embraces his wife, and they become one flesh" (Genesis 2:24). In this passage, sex is intended to seal the bond between two people. When counseling couples whose marriage seems to lack intimacy, we regularly recommend having sex. Paul encourages this practice in 1 Corinthians 7:5: "Don't refuse to meet each other's needs unless you both agree for a short period of time to devote yourselves to prayer. Then come back together again so that Satan might not tempt you because of your lack of self-control." Sex is meant to bond two people in a marriage.

The science of sex backs this up. During arousal and intimacy, a chemical is released in the brain called oxytocin, which increases the feelings of bonding and pleasure. This is the same drug released when a mother holds her baby; it is intended to increase the connection between two people, and that happens during sex. Scripture gives us a more romantic way of saying it: "May your spring be blessed. Rejoice in the wife of your youth. She is a lovely deer, a graceful doe. Let her breasts intoxicate you all the time; always be drunk on her love" (Proverbs 5:18-19). In biblical times or today, such a bond is not meant to be broken.

The unbroken bond between a man and woman in Scripture is called marriage. At weddings we say that Jesus "graced a wedding at Cana of Galilee," referring to events described in John 2. We say this because Jesus not only attended a marriage but also reiterated the need for high expectations of each other when it comes to marriage. In Jesus' day, like ours, divorce was a fact of life, and while Jesus offered grace and forgiveness, he also mourned the divorce rate:

> They said, "Moses allowed a man to write a divorce certificate and to divorce his wife." Jesus said to them, "He wrote this

commandment for you because of your unyielding hearts. At the beginning of creation, God made them male and female. Because of this, a man should leave his father and mother and be joined together with his wife, and the two will be one flesh. So they are no longer two but one flesh. Therefore, humans must not pull apart what God has put together." (Mark 10:4-9)

Jesus knows we are broken people with "unyielding hearts," but in this passage he reminds us that marriage will last until death. Sex and physical intimacy are crucial aspects of the bond that connect two people for a lifetime as they serve God and learn to love God, together.

But if all that happens in sex and marriage is enjoyable bonding intimacy, then why would there need to be any religious restrictions around it at all? Because Christian marriage is about something more. Sex and marriage have goals beyond intimacy and bonding, and it is these goals that give Christian marriage an additional dimension.

One of the goals for sex and marriage in Scripture is procreation. The first commandment to man and woman in the first chapter of Genesis is to "Be fertile and multiply; fill the earth and master it" (Genesis 1:28). The logic of sex and marriage in the story of Scripture is that a couple bonded in marriage would have children and raise their children to love and serve God. One of the most poignant moments in the Old Testament comes from Joshua, the man who took over from Moses in leading the Israelites to the Promised Land. Joshua stood before the Israelites and said, "Choose today whom you will serve. Choose the gods whom your ancestors served beyond the Euphrates or the gods of the Amorites in whose land you live. But my family and I will serve the LORD" (Joshua 24:15). Joshua understood that his role was to perpetuate the lineage of those that followed the God of Abraham, Isaac, Jacob, and Moses, and that would be done through his family and more specifically his children.

Of course, not every married couple is able to or is called to procreate, but every couple is meant to grow in serving and loving God. This was expressed well in Gary Thomas's book *Sacred Marriage*, which had the very descriptive subtitle, *What If God Designed Marriage to Make Us Holy More Than to Make Us Happy?* Such a sentiment is seen clearly in the book of Ephesians, which advises husbands and wives to "submit to each other out of reverence for Christ.... husbands, love your wives, just as Christ loved the church and gave himself for her. He did this in order to make her holy" (Ephesians 5:21, 25-26). Like Christ with the church, the husband is meant to live his life married to his wife in such a way as to help make her holy.

The principle of marriage is mutual submission so that we might each learn how to love each other better. Learning to love our spouses makes us better able to understand what love is and to live it in this lifetime. Our spouses certainly know us and our flaws better than anybody, and if we are committed to loving God together we can come closer to being the person God calls us to be.

The Christian approach to sex and marriage is countercultural, in that it goes against the current trend. In our culture, sex is primarily about what pleasure we can get and give. In a Christian marriage, sex is about how we give ourselves to someone else so that we might be forever bonded as we commit to living holy lives together.

Reclaiming Celibacy

Before we can move on, it is important to spend a few moments considering that it's possible to live a full life without sex. Before Arthur met his wife, he went on a date with a woman who was shocked that he would refrain from having sex until marriage. She asked, "How do you live?" Implicit in her question was the idea that a full life requires sex. This is not the story that we find in Scripture. Paul, at least, thought that refraining from sex and marriage for the whole of one's life is a valid option: "I want you to be free from concerns. A man who isn't married is concerned about the Lord's concerns—how he can please the Lord. But a married man is concerned about the world's concerns—how he can please his wife" (1 Corinthians 7:32-33).

Our culture tells us that we are defined by our gender or sexuality. Those are important qualities, but the Christian story is that we are defined by God. Consider reclaiming celibacy either in a temporary phase when you're single or perhaps even as a permanent act of submission to God. This is the witness of Arthur's wife, Becky. She went to Baylor University, where most of her friends were married during or soon after college. In college and for almost a decade after, Becky was without a husband. During those ten years, she wanted a husband and children, but the time for that had not yet come. Now Becky looks back on that time as a gift. She was able to invest in relationships with great roommates. Through a Bible study, she was a mentor for inner-city girls. Those and other great experiences were only possible because she learned to be defined not by her sexual or marital status, but by God. She made important investments in the lives of others by claiming the gift of celibacy. Both sex and the lack of sex can be gifts.

A Place of Wisdom

Sexual issues are at the core of debates within Christianity and between Christianity and the wider culture. From premarital sex to homosexuality to birth control, disagreements about sex have separated churches and families. This is not the place to detail those debates; let us simply say that people on all sides should remember Jesus' approach to sex: high expectations and high grace. Sex, marriage, and family have a purpose in this life, but sex, marriage, and family are not the only purpose of this life.

How do we conduct conversations about sex in our churches? When our churches and Sunday school classes disagree about sexual matters, is there a place of common ground? Can we come to a place of wisdom about the purpose of sex, even as we disagree about who should have it when? Is there a way to offer grace without judgment to people we disagree with, while at the same time maintaining high expectations?

Real wisdom means following Jesus. He found a middle way of accepting others unconditionally while at the same time expecting more from them on sexual matters. If our culture is trying to imagine a world with a robust sexual and family life in which Jesus and churches are irrelevant, such an attempt will fail. Jesus offers us the path to a full life, and it is only through following him that we will have a chance of holding our society and our church together.

Rapid Response

In a coffee shop, your non-Christian friend says, "Okay, I don't want a long and complicated answer, but tell me this: Why does God care what people do in their own beds?"

You might answer, "We often make the mistake of thinking we can separate our sex lives from the rest of ourselves, but it's not true. Who we are in our most intimate moments can bless or ruin marriages and lives. God has a vision for the whole world to be good. That means he has high hopes for our sex lives, but also grace when we mess up."

7.
Was Jesus' Resurrection Real?

7.
Was Jesus' Resurrection Real?

Christ is risen! He is risen, indeed!

On Easter, the most important day of the year for Christians, the traditional greeting is the declaration of a historical claim. All of Christianity hangs upon this one piece of information, or, as Paul says in 1 Corinthians 15:17, "If Christ hasn't been raised, then your faith is worthless." For Christians, the Resurrection is the most important moment in the history of the world, and yet to our world today it seems an impossible and absurd story. Some may even think it sounds like a fanciful children's story.

Recently a friend recounted a traumatic conversation with her daughter: "[I was] tucking her in and it came ... 'Is Santa real? A boy at my table told me it's your parents giving you presents. Oh, and they said the tooth fairy isn't real, the Easter bunny isn't real, and all those things are just made up by grown-ups.'"

Notice how quickly one lost fantasy gives way to another. Her daughter had woken up that morning believing in Santa Claus, the tooth fairy, and the Easter bunny. She had been brought up on those stories—Santa climbing down every chimney in the world in one night, the tooth fairy magically knowing when she loses a tooth, the Easter bunny bringing baskets of eggs and candy. In one moment, a boy at her table caused her to question everything. It would only be a matter of time until she discovered that the boy at her table was right.

With all the other fairy tales destroyed, how could she grow up to think that the story of Jesus is the one that is true?

In our family, we maintain the pretense of a belief in Santa Claus by saying that we believe in the "spirit of Santa Claus." We continue the practice because we like the story and the tradition. Many people who grew up in a Christian family continue to go to church for the same reason. In this skeptical age, the resurrection of Jesus seems as unbelievable as Santa Claus, but we like the tradition and the nostalgia so we keep a nominal faith in both. We believe the symbolism but not the reality.

In order for us to believe that either Santa Claus or Jesus' resurrection is real, we must suspend what we understand to be the basic rules of the world. There is no way that Santa can fly a sled piloted by reindeer, and there is no way that a dead person can come back to life.

In fact, death tops the list of incurable diseases. We can be cured of cancer and Ebola, but our mortality simply can't be cured—only postponed. Doctors and pharmaceutical companies have found amazing ways to delay death, but they only delay the inevitable. Death is ahead for all of us. As Daniel Defoe wrote in his book *The Political History of the Devil*, "Things as certain as Death and Taxes, can be more firmly believ'd,"[1] meaning that death and taxes are the most constant things in this world.

And yet, the foundational claim of the Christian faith is that there was at least one exception, the resurrection of Jesus. It is said to have occurred about two thousand years ago, meaning that there is no proof. Jesus lived, died, and rose from the dead in an age before video cameras, thermometers, X-rays, MRIs, DNA sequencers, or anything else that would be needed to verify someone's death and resurrection.

If scientific proof of Jesus' resurrection is unavailable, then why do so many believe? The only evidence we have is stories and letters from those who claim to have seen the Resurrection. The challenge for Christians is that these stories of resurrection are not consistent. How many women were at the empty tomb? The Gospel of Mark records three women, but John says only Mary Magdalene was present. What was Jesus' resurrected body like? In Luke, the risen Jesus ate fish, but in John, Jesus suddenly appears in a locked room. Is Jesus' body solid or ghostlike? How are we in a modern and skeptical world to believe contradictory stories from thousands of years ago without proof?

That little girl who went to school and learned the truth about the tooth fairy and Santa Claus learned an important lesson: some things are just made up by adults. Is Jesus' resurrection made up too? Can we follow Jesus if the story about Easter isn't true? What if everything else about Jesus in the Bible is true and just this one part is false—would it matter?

A Story with Consequences for Us

Christians believe that Easter is the crucial part of the story. Christianity is founded upon the historical claim that Jesus rose from the grave, making it either the most significant fact in the history of the world or a complete sham. Eternity and salvation hang upon this claim, and Christians believe that each person must decide whether or not to believe. According to the story of Jesus' resurrection in Matthew, the final instruction that the risen Jesus gave his followers was that they were to "go and make disciples of all nations, baptizing them in the name of the Father and of the Son and of the Holy Spirit" (Matthew 28:19). The disciples did just that, moving across the known world and asking people to choose for themselves whether they wanted to be baptized in the name of the risen Jesus.

The Bible actually tells the story of one of the first people who was in a position to choose, not based on proof but on the story. His name was Cornelius and he was a centurion, an officer in the Roman army. Cornelius had heard that there were witnesses to the Resurrection and so sent his servants to fetch Peter. When the servants arrived, Peter asked, "Why have you come?"

They replied, "We've come on behalf of Cornelius, a centurion and righteous man, a God-worshipper who is well-respected by all Jewish people. A holy angel directed him to summon you to his house and to hear what you have to say" (Acts 10:21-22).

Peter went to Cornelius and told his story:

> "You know about Jesus of Nazareth.... We are witnesses of everything he did, both in Judea and in Jerusalem. They killed him by hanging him on a tree, but God raised him up on the third day and allowed him to be seen, not by everyone but by us. We are witnesses whom God chose beforehand, who ate

and drank with him after God raised him from the dead...."
While Peter was still speaking, the Holy Spirit fell on everyone
who heard the word. (Acts 10:38-42; 44)

Cornelius heard Peter's testimony and was convinced it was true. His family
was all immediately baptized and became disciples of Jesus. All of this occurred
simply because Peter shared his eyewitness account. Cornelius did not make
the decision based on scientific truth but on whether or not he believed Peter's
witness. Cornelius sought out Peter's testimony because he knew that this
claim, if true, was the most important fact in history.

C. S. Lewis put it this way: "Christianity, if false, is of *no* importance,
and if true, of infinite importance. The one thing it cannot be is moderately
important."[2] Cornelius believed the same thing. If Peter was telling the truth
and Jesus Christ rose from the grave, then salvation and eternal life were offered
to him if he would be baptized. If Peter was mistaken or lying, then baptism
was worthless and Cornelius should move on to other things. The only foolish
thing to do would be to adopt a nominal faith. Jesus' resurrection is a binary
choice: either it happened or it didn't.

We believe with Lewis in the importance of the Resurrection, but we also
believe that Christianity makes the world better even if the Resurrection
never happened. We add this observation because some atheist authors have
suggested that Christianity is in fact detrimental, or, as Christopher Hitchens
wrote, "Religion poisons everything."[3] This is claim is absurd to us; faith has
brought benefits to countless lives. Some of those benefits are:

- *Community*. Humans are communal creatures, desperate for a place
  to call home and to be known by others. Having friends who feel like
  family can allow a person to flourish. In our ministries, we have seen
  people who have found real and lasting community in the church.
- *Common purpose*. Christian communities provide people with a
  direction in life. Proverbs 29:18 says: "When there's no vision, the
  people get out of control, but whoever obeys instruction is happy."
  A common faith brings people together for a common purpose that is
  valuable, no matter the details of the theology.

- *Care for the poor*. Christians, following the example of Jesus, are expected to care for the poor and vulnerable. This was true of even the earliest Christians. One non-Christian Roman emperor, Julian the Apostate, was frustrated because those who followed Jesus were not only taking care of their own poor but were caring for the sick and needy who were not Christian. He wrote to a high-priest, "The Hellenic religion does not prosper as I desire… For it is disgraceful that, when no Jew ever has to beg, and the impious Galilaeans support not only their own poor but ours as well, all men see that our people lack aid from us."[4] The present-day Pope Francis has continued to speak out for the poor. In a 2014 speech, he stated that people who criticize the church for its work "don't understand that love for the poor is at the center of the gospel."[5]

These benefits make Christianity valuable even if there were no Resurrection. In the end, though, the Christian message is not just that people are made better by following Jesus, but that salvation and eternal life are possible. C. S. Lewis was correct—the Resurrection either happened or it didn't. We all have the opportunity to choose what we believe took place that first Easter morning, when the disciples said the grave was empty and Jesus rose from the dead.

Logical Possibilities

Before we discuss the logical possibilities of Jesus' resurrection, we must define what it means to say that Jesus rose from the dead. The most important point to make here is that resurrection is different from resuscitation, in which a dead body is brought back to life only to die once again. In other words, the rules of mortality still hold, meaning that no matter how many times people are resuscitated they still will die one day. Their bodies have not been changed or healed, merely brought back. Resurrection, on the other hand, is the claim of a transformed body. The disciples said that even though Jesus endured the whipping and a crucifixion, he appeared to them a few days later. That body would never again die. That is what Christians mean by resurrection.

With that definition in mind, let's explore some logical options regarding Jesus' resurrection.

Option 1: Jesus never existed.

This is the most unlikely of all options. The argument sometimes given for this possibility is that there is no archeological evidence for Jesus, that the only proof of Jesus' existence comes from stories of those who knew him and the impact of the religion that began after his death. In fact, there is as much evidence for the existence of Jesus as for other ancient figures such as Socrates. No archeological proof exists of either person, but we have writings from those who knew them and followed their teachings. These writings put Jesus in a different category from those described in Greek and Roman mythology— gods that people had never met. Jesus left too much of an impact for us to believe that he never existed.

Option 2: Jesus' didn't die on the cross.

This option is also extraordinarily unlikely, but it does provide an explanation for how Jesus was alive the week after his crucifixion. This option is unlikely because the stories are clear that Jesus died and the powers that be wanted it that way. The Jewish leaders and the Roman governor had an interest in eliminating popular leaders such as Jesus, who were threats to lead a revolution. In fact, the Gospel of John writes that Jesus was "already dead" (John 19:33) when the soldiers came to hurry along the process of dying so they could get the body down before nightfall, the beginning of Sabbath, as the religious leaders had requested. Death is the expected result of crucifixion. There is at least one recorded story of a person surviving crucifixion, but that person's crucifixion was interrupted and the man revived under the care of a doctor.[6] This did not happen to Jesus; the religious leaders of the day, the Roman authorities, and the disciples all believed that Jesus had died on the cross.

Perhaps the more telling point is that Christianity would not have been launched the way it was if Jesus merely had survived execution. He would have been weak from blood loss and torture and would have looked like a beaten down and failed messiah. Instead, the disciples were willing to die for him and undergo their own torture. Barely surviving execution does not explain the actions of the disciples and the creation of Christianity.

Option 3: Jesus died, but someone stole his body.

This is the option that, on the surface, explains the most without resorting to a supernatural explanation. Jesus died, and his body was placed in a tomb on a Friday. His body was not discovered to be missing until Sunday morning, leaving Friday night and all day Saturday for someone to steal the body. This leads to the question: Who is the "someone" who stole the body? And if the body was stolen, why were the disciples willing to die to proclaim that they had seen him alive after that weekend? There seem to be two possibilities:

(a) Jesus' disciples stole the body, buried it elsewhere, and then lied about the Resurrection. This is the simplest possibility, explaining what happened to the body and why Christianity took off the way it did. In order to pull off this deception, the disciples would have needed a large group of coconspirators, all of whom were willing to die for a lie. The actual stealing of the body could have been accomplished by a few individuals, but Paul in 1 Corinthians 15 names a whole host of people who witnessed Jesus' resurrection. Getting all those people to agree to the lie is unlikely. Even more unlikely is that the coconspirators such as Peter and the other disciples would be willing to undergo imprisonment, ridicule, and death for something they knew to be a lie.

(b) Someone else stole the body, and the disciples either lied or mass-hallucinated. The obvious question here is who else besides the disciples would have stolen the body? The Jewish leaders and Roman government had a vested interest in Jesus' death and would not have stolen his body. Even if they had, they would have brought out the body as proof of his death once the disciples claimed resurrection. If some other person or group had stolen the body, then why would the disciples claim he was risen if they knew the body might reappear someday? And it would be a remarkable and unlikely coincidence that someone else would have stolen the body while a large group of disciples underwent a mass-hallucination.

Options 1, 2, and 3 are the most likely without a supernatural explanation. Yet none of these explain why the disciples were willing to die for their claim that Jesus had risen from the dead.

Option 4: Jesus' resurrection happened.

The last option is that the disciples were telling the truth: Jesus' body was not in the tomb because he had risen from the dead. This option explains everything except, of course, for the improbability of resurrection. The problem is that we have no proof; all we have is testimony. This is as true now as it was for Cornelius two thousand years ago. He stood face to face with Peter, pondering the same possibilities that we have identified above. Was Peter lying? Was he simply hallucinating? In the end Cornelius believed him, because as improbable as resurrection is, it is the answer that made the most sense to him. Sherlock Holmes once famously said, "How often have I said to you that when you have eliminated the impossible, whatever remains, however improbable, must be the truth?"[7] The only story that convincingly explains the actions and subsequent lives of the disciples is the one they told and believed: Jesus rose from the dead.

The Disciples Believed in the Resurrection of Jesus

Belief in Jesus' resurrection hinges on the testimony of the men and women who became disciples. We commit a huge historical error when we assume that they were fools who simply didn't know better. We think of ourselves and our age as scientific, and therefore of every other age as primitive. But in the book of John, when Mary Magdalene went to the tomb, we find that her response was reasonable even by today's standards. When confronted by angels who asked why she was crying, Mary responded, "They have taken away my Lord, and I don't know where they've put him." Her first rational thought was that someone had stolen Jesus' body. She continued to believe that until she had proof of Jesus standing in front of her. She and the other followers of Jesus were not fools; they just had an almost unbelievable story to tell.

Christianity is not a story written by one person but a consistent witness by a group of people. That consistent witness is recorded in what we call the New Testament, the section of the Bible written after the time of Jesus. The most comprehensive accounts are in the first four books, called the Gospels. The first three Gospels (Matthew, Mark, and Luke) are the most similar. Some places in Luke and Matthew, for example, are word–for-word identical to sections in the Book of Mark. This is important because when historians try to prove a story that happened so long ago, they look for independent accounts. Because Matthew, Mark, and Luke are very similar, they lose some of their power as three independent witnesses. Their similarity makes the fourth Gospel, John, very important: The Gospel of John appears to be an independent witness who agrees with the basic message that Jesus rose from the dead. All the Gospels have inconsistencies (even Matthew, Mark, and Luke), but they do not disagree on that one important point.

Other sources besides the four Gospels provide supporting testimony in the New Testament. The Book of Acts, for example, is written by the same author as the Gospel of Luke. It tells of the story of the early church and of the disciples who witnessed Jesus' resurrection and testified to it even at the point of death. The first to die for Jesus was a man named Stephen, whose job it was to care for the widows in the early Christian community. Stephen was put on trial and gave a sermon proclaiming that Jesus stood at the right hand of God in heaven. As Stephen was being stoned, he prayed, "Lord Jesus, accept my life" (Acts 7:59). Stephen was part of a community who believed in Jesus and his resurrection so strongly that they were willing to die for him.

Participating in the murder of Stephen was a man named Saul, who would later become the great Apostle Paul, a key leader of the early church. Paul wrote many of the letters in the New Testament and was another independent witness to the actions and beliefs of Jesus' early disciples. He began to follow Jesus much later than the others, so you might think he is an odd choice to provide us with proof of the Resurrection. Yet it is precisely his later conversion that makes him special. We are told in the Book of Acts that Saul participated in the stoning of Stephen and later, while traveling on a road to Damascus, met the risen Christ. Saul was a persecutor of the Christians and then, as Paul, became their greatest evangelist. Here is his most famous passage about the proof of the Resurrection:

> I passed on to you as most important what I also received: Christ died for our sins in line with the scriptures, he was buried, and he rose on the third day in line with the scriptures. He appeared to Cephas, then to the Twelve, and then he appeared to more than five hundred brothers and sisters at once—most of them are still alive to this day, though some have died. Then he appeared to James, then to all the apostles, and last of all he appeared to me, as if I were born at the wrong time.
>
> (1 Corinthians 15:3-8)

Paul's witness is consistent with the stories we have in the four Gospels and the Book of Acts, the same basic story that is either explicit or implied in every book of the New Testament.

The letters of Peter, for example, explicitly include in the introduction, "You have been born anew into a living hope through the resurrection of Jesus Christ from the dead" (1 Peter 1:3). By contrast, the Book of Jude only implies the Resurrection, by saying, "But you, dear friends: build each other up on the foundation of your most holy faith, pray in the Holy Spirit, keep each other in the love of God, wait for the mercy of our Lord Jesus Christ, who will give you eternal life. Have mercy on those who doubt" (Jude 20-22). The only reason people would call Jesus *Lord* and believe in eternal life was because they believed that Jesus' body was not stolen and didn't rot in a grave.

The best explanation for the existence of Christianity is that the disciples were telling the truth. They believed that Jesus rose from the dead, and the example of their faith and actions is our best proof.

In the introduction to this book, we briefly quoted David Bentley Hart on the topic of Christianity. Here is the rest of that passage:

> Christianity is the only major faith built entirely around a single historical claim. It is, however, a claim quite unlike any other ever made, as any perceptive and scrupulous historian must recognize. Certainly it bears no resemblance to the vague fantasies of witless enthusiasts or to the cunning machinations of opportunistic charlatans. It is the report of men and women who had suffered the devastating defeat of their beloved master's death, but who in a very short time were proclaiming an immediate experience of his living presence beyond the tomb, and who were, it seems, willing to suffer privation, imprisonment, torture, and death rather than deny that experience.[8]

A Faith That Will Last

Peter and the other disciples never abandoned their faith in Jesus. His resurrection was not a fairy tale for them; it was not something that grown-ups made up. They witnessed a life-changing event, then sacrificed everything to tell others about it. This makes the story of Jesus' resurrection different from other stories, even those in Scripture. Only Moses could say whether the burning bush really was on fire. Only Abraham knew if God really had said he would be the father of many nations. But multiple witnesses testified that Jesus' resurrection took place.

We cannot leave this chapter saying only that out of the logical possibilities, the disciples' testimony about the Resurrection might be true. That may be the most cautious, fact-based answer, but it doesn't lead us to a place of wisdom.

The Resurrection is of no value for our lives if it might be true. It has value only if we learn to have faith that it is true. Something must happen within us, as it happened to Peter, the first leader of Christianity and the man who gave his testimony to Cornelius. Even before Jesus died, Peter had been told he would lead the church, and yet when Jesus was arrested, Peter's will was broken. He denied three times that night that he was a follower of Jesus. Something must have happened after that to give him confidence to lead the church after his leader was executed. The best explanation for what happened is that Peter came face to face with Jesus after the Resurrection and, as a result, spent the rest of his life with a strong faith. This is the story that Christians over the years have told, and it is what we call wisdom.

Faith is available to us, just as it was to Cornelius just a few weeks after Jesus' resurrection. Cornelius did not have scientific proof; he only had Peter's story. For Christians, believing in the possibility of Jesus' resurrection is not enough; the only way to achieve true hope is to reach a point where we believe and trust in the Resurrection as a glorious, living fact.

Peter, Paul, James, Cornelius, and a multitude of others believed in the resurrection and had faith because of it. Out of all the possibilities of what happened on that first Easter morning, we choose to trust those who walked with Jesus, fled when they saw him die, and still proclaimed to their death that Jesus had risen from the dead. Faith in this story brings true wisdom and hope.

Rapid Response

Your non-Christian friend says, "Okay, I don't want a long, complicated answer, but tell me this: What proof is there that Jesus actually rose from the dead? Your faith depends on it, but all you have are stories."

You might answer, "You are right—all we have are stories, the stories of those who followed Jesus, watched him die, saw him raised from the dead, and told everyone about him. There might be other possibilities of what happened to Jesus, but none that make as much sense for me. I choose to believe those who were willing to die for their truth so that you and I might have hope."

8.
Why Do Christians Disagree About So Many Things?

8.
Why Do Christians Disagree About So Many Things?

Jesus set a high standard for Christian unity. In John 17:18-23, we read that Jesus prayed to God for his disciples, saying,

> As you sent me into the world, so I have sent them into the world. I made myself holy on their behalf so that they also would be made holy in the truth. I'm not praying only for them but also for those who believe in me because of their word. I pray they will be one, Father, just as you are in me and I am in you. I pray that they also will be in us, so that the world will believe that you sent me. I've given them the glory that you gave me so that they can be one just as we are one. I'm in them and you are in me so that they will be made perfectly one. Then the world will know that you sent me and that you have loved them just as you loved me.

That vision of unity was tested very early in the Christian community, as the disciples who spoke Greek felt discriminated against by those who spoke Aramaic. Called the Hellenists and the Hebrews, the two groups resolved their conflict by appointing seven people to handle the administrative tasks in ways that preserved unity.

The Book of Acts goes on to describe other tensions that developed in places such as Corinth. There, Paul used the metaphor of the body and the appeal to love in urging Christian unification. Later, in his letter to the Ephesians, Paul wrote,

> Therefore, as a prisoner for the Lord, I encourage you to live as people worthy of the call you received from God. Conduct yourselves with all humility, gentleness, and patience. Accept each other with love, and make an effort to preserve the unity of the Spirit with the peace that ties you together. You are one body and one spirit, just as God also called you in one hope. There is one Lord, one faith, one baptism, and one God and Father of all, who is over all, through all, and in all.
>
> (Ephesians 4:1-6)

During the fourth century, leaders of the church met in two councils, one at Nicaea in A.D. 325 and one at Constantinople in 381. These two meetings produced the Nicene Creed, the third article of which says, in part, "We believe in the one holy catholic [all-embracing or universal] and apostolic church."[1] But there is an even bolder claim for unity. In 2 Corinthians 5:19, Paul suggests that "God was reconciling the world to himself through Christ" and that believers are now ambassadors of reconciliation. In another book, using breathtaking imagery, Paul enunciates the vision of world unity in Christ:

> The Son is the image of the invisible God, the one who is first over all creation, Because all things were created by him: both in the heavens and on the earth, the things that are visible and the things that are invisible. Whether they are thrones or powers, or rulers or authorities, all things were created through him and for him. He existed before all things, and all things are held together in him. He is the head of the body, the church, who is the beginning, the one who is firstborn from among the dead so that he might occupy the first place in everything. Because all the fullness of God was pleased to live in him, and he reconciled all things to himself through him—whether

things on earth or in the heavens. He brought peace through the blood of his cross. (Colossians 1:15-20)

Christianity's self-understanding is that it should be a unified community of believers who in turn are serving God's purpose of unifying the whole world for God.

The Question

Christianity began as a small movement within Judaism soon after Christ died and rose from the dead. To resolve disagreements, leaders of the church met in councils that produced creeds intended to unify the church. Through such decisions, the church charted a course to resolve the questions at hand, but frequently there was a side effect: those who disagreed formed separate churches, all of which claimed to follow Christ. After two thousand years there are many Christian denominations.

In 2011, the Pew Research Center identified forty-one thousand Christian organizations, most of which might be labeled as denominations.[2] In most United States communities, the denominational pattern has led to multiple Christian congregations representing those denominations (as well as other churches that refer to themselves as nondenominational). Denominationalism was exported to Africa, South America, and Asia, so that in almost every country where Christianity exists, there are multiple expressions of it.

So much for unity.

Why do Christians disagree about so many things?

Some History

One way to answer that question is to describe how Christianity changed to become the very diverse group of denominations that it is today. Sometimes the denominations are grouped into major families. Let's take a look at how those major families came to exist.

For the first thousand years of Christianity, there were some divisions over issues about the doctrine of the Trinity and the two natures of Christ. Other disagreements arose over images and the best way to describe the role of Mary, the mother of Jesus. Yet, by the year A.D. 1000 most Christians were united under the leadership of bishops in the major cities along with five patriarchs. These patriarchs were the bishops of cities who exercised leadership over regions, with the Bishop of Rome (the Pope) being given the role of first among the patriarchs. Ecumenical councils met several times to settle significant disputes, and there were tensions among different regions of the church. There also were different understandings of how much authority was granted to the Bishop of Rome, and these different understandings were increasing over time.

In 1054 the differences between the Greek-speaking Eastern part of the church and the Latin-speaking Western part of the church widened to produce a formal split. Because the church still sought unity, each side claimed to be the "one, holy, catholic and apostolic church," which meant those on the other side were not truly Christians. Four patriarchs became part of the Orthodox Church, and the Pope became the leader of the Roman Catholic Church.

This split between the churches centered around the authority of the Pope, the Holy Spirit's relationship to God the Father, and issues involving worship and liturgy. Outside the church, the Roman Empire had also split between the East, centered in Constantinople, and the West, centered in Rome, and resultant cultural and secular factors also contributed to the church split. Both churches valued apostolic succession, the view that bishops are ordained by other bishops in a line going back to the apostles.

Within Western Europe, Roman Catholicism faced a major split during the sixteenth century. As the Holy Roman Empire became weaker, nation-states developed, and different languages replaced Latin. The invention of the printing press in the mid-fifteenth century sharpened the question of whether the Bible should be translated into the languages of the people, and theological questions about faith and good works took on new urgency. This issue and other factors led to the Protestant Reformation.

One key turning point was Martin Luther's nailing a list of questions and propositions, called "The 95 Theses," to the door of the Wittenberg Castle church in 1517. Luther translated the Bible into German and rallied the German princes and people to resist the Pope's authority in religious matters. Elsewhere in Europe, John Calvin and others led movements that created the

Reformed churches, while a group led by Ulrich Zwingli taught a different understanding of baptism, restricting it to those who could profess faith in Christ for themselves. Since all other churches practiced infant baptism as well as believer's baptism, this group was called "Anabaptist," meaning baptized again.

Viewed together, the Lutheran, Reformed, and Anabaptist churches were called Protestants, since they were protesting against perceived problems within the Roman Catholic Church. In England, the church took steps to restrict the Pope's authority and to adopt some Protestant doctrines while still retaining apostolic succession and many Catholic practices, resulting in the Church of England. Methodism arose in the eighteenth century as a renewal movement within the Church of England.

A crucial trend developed in Europe during the seventeenth century. Prior to that time, every political unit had practiced only one form of Christianity, with the king, queen, or prince, and all the citizens sharing that same form. But the seventeenth-century wars of religion caused great harm throughout Europe, and as a way of avoiding additional conflicts, different churches were allowed worship and function in the same country. England was the most advanced regarding this pattern after 1689: the Church of England was established, but Congregationalists, Baptists, and Presbyterians were tolerated. The word denomination came to describe these independent Christian bodies.

The nineteenth century saw a great missionary movement from Europe and America to places being colonized in Africa, Asia, and Latin America. Though earlier missionaries had gone to many of these places—notably Roman Catholics to European colonies—the number of missionaries and their success in planting churches grew exponentially. The new missionaries naturally started churches of their own denominations in the new countries. Thus, a country such as Nigeria would soon have indigenous churches with Roman Catholic, Anglican, Baptist, Lutheran, and several Methodist bodies.

The nineteenth century also saw further divisions within existing churches. Methodists in America split over racism, slavery, the power of bishops, and the doctrine of the Holy Spirit. The Pentecostal movement began in the early twentieth century, as people experienced powerful gifts of the Holy Spirit.

America during the nineteenth century saw the rise of new churches that came from Christianity but no longer affirmed the doctrine of the Trinity. The Unitarian movement began from Congregationalist roots, and the Church of Jesus Christ of Latter Day Saints (Mormons) arose from the leadership of Joseph Smith. While such groups often are associated with Christianity and sometimes claim to be Christian, most Christians believe that affirmation of the truths expressed by the Nicene Creed is a requirement of Christian identity.

Four Characteristics of Christianity

As we have seen, one way to answer this chapter's question is to look at history. Another way is to describe four fundamental characteristics of Christianity and how they contribute to the disagreements among denominations.

First, Christians believe that God became a human being when the second person of the Trinity was born as Jesus of Nazareth. The infinite became finite. The universal became local. The spiritual took on human flesh. This process was called the Incarnation, where God became human in order to save humanity from our sins. God became a first-century Jew speaking Aramaic and Greek and practicing the religion of first-century Judiasm. The intention for the Christian movement was to help all of humanity, each and every person, to be reconciled to God and worship him as revealed in Christ; the intention was not to make everyone become an Aramaic-speaking Jew in order to be saved. The amazing events of Pentecost (Acts 2), just weeks after Jesus' ascension, demonstrated the power of the Spirit to help people hear the gospel in their own languages. As Christianity spread, it adapted to the many cultures in which the gospel was taking root. The New Testament was translated into multiple languages. Churches were built on the sites of pagan holy places. Key Christian holy days were adapted from special days in local cultures. The process of helping widely varying groups of people come to Christ meant that Christianity took on different forms in different parts of the world.

This adaptability was essential to Christianity's success, but it also created tensions among the various expressions of the faith. How much adaptation was permissible? What were the nonnegotiable aspects that had to be maintained in new Christian communities? What in the new culture could be carried over into

Christian culture, and what must be changed when one was baptized? Some diversity was welcomed and expected, but there were inevitably disagreements about what Christian unity requires. These tensions were already visible in the New Testament and have continued to the present day.

A second characteristic of Christianity was the formation of a community, the church. Community requires leadership, and the twelve apostles chosen by Jesus were the original community leaders. (Judas was replaced by another eyewitness to Jesus' ministry.) Over time, the leadership in each community was vested in a bishop, who was seen as the successor to the apostles. All the bishops as a group formed the leadership team for the church. They gathered in councils for the entire church on seven occasions in the first thousand years. As we have seen, the church initially was led by five patriarchs, then split into East and West, with the Western church led by the Pope. The Reformation led to further fracturing about the governance of the church. Many Protestants did not value the apostolic succession of bishops as the authorities and sought to substitute the authority of Scripture for the authority of the Pope. But people read Scripture in different ways, and with no final authoritative interpreter, different denominations developed different structures of authority. Some vested authority in the ordained elders, who were called presbyters, while others gave authority to the lay members of the church, others to local congregations, and others to various mixtures of laity, clergy, and bishops.

A third characteristic of Christianity was the belief that God had inspired authoritative writings to guide the church's message and practice. As we saw in Chapter 5, those writings were originally the Jewish Bible. Over time, the Gospels and letters of Paul were seen to be inspired Scripture, and finally in the fourth century the New Testament contents were formed and agreed upon. Over time, new challenges arose and church councils were called to decide how best to interpret Scripture. For example, if Jesus of Nazareth is truly divine, how do we believe in the one God taught in Deuteronomy 6:4? If Jesus is both fully human and fully divine, does he have one nature or two? As scientific knowledge of the world progressed, further challenges developed, and the tensions between faith and reason increased. United Methodists, for example, have addressed this issue by saying that while Scripture is primary, reason, tradition, and experience can also be used to shape faith and practice. Even within that tradition, people disagree about how much weight should be given to each of the four authorities.

A fourth characteristic of Christianity is its relationship to secular government. Before 325, Christianity was one of many religions in a diverse empire, but it still had to negotiate the Roman state religion and its requirements, which led to persecution of Christians. But from the time of Emperor Constantine until the middle ages, Christianity developed a close relationship with the political leaders of the empires and kingdoms where it was located. The Pope sometimes crowned the emperor, and the Byzantine emperor sometimes chose the Patriarch of Constantinople. Since the Reformation, Christian denominations have adopted a variety of relationships between themselves and the governments of their nations. Some remain formally established, such as the Church of England; others refuse to engage in secular politics or even to pay taxes; and many others seek influence and are willing to be closely aligned with secular governments. As we can see from these varied approaches, Christians disagree about the role they should play in the larger society.

Disagreement Among Denominations

The world is rapidly changing, and Christianity's response is a matter of disagreement among denominations, as well as within them. One major issue is the role of women in the church. Though women have played important parts throughout Christian history, the clergy and bishops traditionally were all male. The New Testament has some verses that appear to prohibit women from speaking in church or exercising authority over men, while other verses refer to women speaking and being leaders in early Christian communities. For centuries women could become nuns but could not be ordained as priests or bishops. Beginning in the nineteenth century, some churches began to ordain women, and now most Protestant churches do so. Some, however, do not ordain women, and the Roman Catholic Church maintains the traditional restrictions. Also, even among those churches that ordain women as clergy and bishops, there is some disagreement about whether their formal acceptance has led to true equality.

Another major issue is Christianity's role in the wider culture. In Europe and the Americas, Christianity traditionally was the dominant force in the culture, shaping holidays, education, family life, and morality. As the process of secularization has progressed, however, Christian convictions about marriage, sexual relationships, divorce, racism, and prayer have been challenged. Changing patterns of technology, music, and communication have caused disagreements about the proper way to worship God.

Some churches have embraced changes in their teaching and worship styles as a way of learning from the culture. They argue that while the gospel doesn't change, the way it is communicated and practiced must change to accomplish God's purposes. Other churches, believing the very nature of Christian witness is threatened by some of the new approaches being advocated, have sought to maintain traditional views, practices, and worship styles. Internal disputes about these matters have caused some churches to divide. The secular media have picked up on the disputes and emphasized them, making Christians appear to be more conflicted and divided than perhaps they are.

Whether or not our differences have been emphasized by the media, Christians must admit that we do disagree. Our disagreements have arisen in part because of Christianity's success in shaping Western culture, which in turn has spawned nation-states, formed colonies, developed modern science, and invented the concept of religious freedom. These changes have opened up opportunities for religious groups to form, divide, and grow.

Of all these changes, the growing trend toward religious freedom and the separation of religion from governmental power has perhaps had the greatest impact. The Reformation destroyed the unity of Christianity in Western Europe. It was followed by the Enlightenment, which helped redefine the relationship of individuals to their communities. One of the key tenets of the Enlightenment was that people should be free from government coercion in matters of religion. The resulting pattern of religious freedom allowed many different religions to take root in Western countries. Within Christianity, the number of denominations multiplied, and groups such as Unitarians and the Church of Jesus Christ of Latter-day Saints (Mormons) moved out of traditional Christianity. Similar processes have led to multiple forms of all major religions.

In such an environment, it is not surprising that Christians disagree. It is more surprising that they have focused as much as they have on unity and agreement.

Seeking Unity

In spite of media claims, Christians are not as divided as many people believe. Christian denominations hold the vast majority of beliefs in common. Most recognize each other's baptisms and regard the members of other churches as Christians. There are significant ways in which local churches, regional groups, and entire denominations work together. Food pantries, thanksgiving worship services, disaster relief projects, and witness for social justice are all ways in which interdenominational cooperation is taking place.

Yet there is division, and it is a hindrance to the gospel. The amount of time Christians spend arguing with each other gives the impression that we don't truly love each other.

Christians should find ways to be more united. There is a heritage upon which to build. People from different denominations have cooperated in many ways through the centuries. In nineteenth-century America, significant levels of interdenominational cooperation were shown in camp meetings, revivals, Sunday schools, theological education, and mission work.

In 1910, a fresh effort at uniting Christians was begun, with an international missionary conference held in Edinburgh, Scotland. Missionaries who had worked in Africa and Asia testified that the disunity of Christians was a hindrance to the gospel. By 1948, the World Council of Churches was formed as the leading agent for Christian unity worldwide. National councils were created in many countries for the same purpose. In the aftermath of World War II, there was a great deal of optimism in Europe and America for reconciling the many divided parts of Christ's body.

The Second Vatican Council, meeting from 1961 to 1965, provided official backing for an increase in the ecumenical involvement of the Roman Catholic Church. Increasing dialogue among different churches has been taking place for more than four decades. Such dialogue identifies the real issues separating the churches, as well as opportunities for growing closer. While the official ecumenical movement has lost momentum during the past fifteen years, the attitude and spirit of ecumenism that it fostered remains strong in many churches. The long-term answer is for Christian to reunite into one visible, global, Christian church.

The spiritual ingredient necessary for such unity is already present in the hearts and minds of many Christians. John Wesley, the founder of Methodism, called the ingredient "catholic spirit." In his sermon of that name, Wesley said that Christians are different people and cannot all think alike. He did point to some essential doctrines, which all Christians can be expected to hold in common. One might suggest that the Nicene Creed is such an essential doctrine. To quit believing in the teachings of the Creed is to quit being a Christian. But there are other beliefs that Wesley described as "matters of opinion." He named modes of worship and infant baptism as two such doctrines, saying that even though we may disagree on matters of opinion, each person should hold a belief on them, because indifference on important issues is not helpful. At the same time, because they are not essential doctrines, it is possible that one might be mistaken on this or that matter. This possibility of error should lead to a certain amount of humility: to be human is to make mistakes, and on matters of opinion one might be wrong.[3] Wesley's friendship with George Whitfield, a Methodist who believed in predestination, was an example of that kind of fellowship and mutual respect.[4]

Wesley taught that catholic or universal spirit is the same as catholic or universal love. It is a belief that people whose hearts are committed to Christ and the basic teachings of the faith should be able to love each other and work together for the benefit of God's kingdom.

Rapid Response

Your non-Christian friend says, "Okay, I don't want a long, complicated answer, but tell me this: Why do Christians disagree about so many things?"

You might respond, "Christians actually agree on the most important things, and we already work together more than most people realize. We really do love each other. But we can do a better job of it, and our witness would be stronger if we were more united. We need to work on that."

Notes

Introduction

1. David Bentley Hart, *Atheist Delusions* (New Haven, CT: Yale University Press, 2010), 11.

1. Can Only One Religion Be True?

1. "Major Religions of the World Ranked by Number of Adherents," accessed May 23, 2015, http://www.adherents.com/Religions_By_Adherents.html. The list also places as the third group "Secular/Nonreligious/Agnostic/Atheist estimated at 1.1 billion. It lists Juche (the North Korean ideology) at 19 million in the tenth spot.
2. Yann Martel, *The Life of Pi* (Boston: Mariner Books/Houghton Mifflin Harcourt, 2012), 28.
3. Kirsten Powers, "Fox News' Highly Reluctant Jesus Follower," *Christianity Today* (October 22, 2013), accessed October 14, 2014, http://www.christianitytoday.com /ct/2013/november/fox-news-highly-reluctant-jesus-follower-kirsten-powers.html.
4. Ibid.
5. Scott J. Jones, *The Wesleyan Way* (Nashville: Abingdon Press, 2013), 51–52.
6. C. S. Lewis, *The Last Battle* (New York: Collier Books, 1970), 164–65.
7. Scott J. Jones, *The Evangelistic Love of God and Neighbor* (Nashville: Abingdon Press, 2003), 21.

2. Why Is There Suffering and Evil?

1. "9/11 Memorial," accessed June 3, 2015, http://www.911memorial.org/faq-about-911.
2. National Weather Service, "Hurricanes in History," accessed June 3, 2015, http://www .nhc.noaa.gov/outreach/history/#katrina.
3. "World War I Fast Fact," CNN, last updated July 11, 2014, accessed June 3, 2015, http:// www.cnn.com/2013/07/09/world/world-war-i-fast-facts/.
4. Charles Tilly, *The Politics of Collective Violence* (Cambridge, UK: Cambridge University Press, 2003), 55.
5. John Wesley, "God's Approbation of His Works," in *The Works of John Wesley,* ed. Albert C. Outler (Nashville: Abingdon Press, 1985), 2:397.
6. Stuart K. Hine, "How Great Thou Art," *The United Methodist Hymnal* (Nashville: United Methodist Publishing House, 1989), #77. Copyright © 1949 and 1953 The Stuart Hine Trust.
7. "How Wolves Change Rivers" accessed March 15, 2015, https://www.youtube.com /watch?v=ysa5OBhXz-Q.

8. Nathan Kilbourne, personal correspondence with author, January 20, 2015.

9. Natalie Sleeth, "Hymn of Promise," *The United Methodist Hymnal* (Nashville: United Methodist Publishing House, 1989), #707. Copyright © 1986 Hope Publishing Co.

3. How Can I Believe in Science and Creation?

1. "It's Science, but Not Necessarily Right," *New York Times*, June 25, 2011, accessed March 16, 2015, http://www.nytimes.com/2011/06/26/opinion/sunday/26ideas.html?_r=0.

2. "A New Generation Expresses Its Skepticism and Frustration with Christianity," Barna Group, accessed June 11, 2015, https://www.barna.org/barna-update/teens-nextgen /94-a-new-generation-expresses-its-skepticism-and-frustration-with-christianity# .VXmDpaZqBz0.

3. De Principiis (Book IV), 16, http://newadvent.org/fathers/04124.htm.

4. Excerpt from *St. Augustine, the Literal Meaning of Genesis*, vol. 1, Ancient Christian Writers, vol. 41, trans. John Hammond Taylor, S.J. (New York: Paulist Press, 1982), accessed June 4, 2015, http://college.holycross.edu/faculty/alaffey/other_files /Augustine-Genesis1.pdf.

5. Article 5, "Of the Sufficiency of the Holy Scriptures for Salvation," The Articles of Religion of The Methodist Church, *The Book of Discipline of The United Methodist Church 2012* (Nashville: The United Methodist Publishing House, 2012), 64.

6. Werner Heisenberg, as cited in Ulrich Hildebrand, "Das Universum - Hinweis auf Gott?" in *Ethos* no 10 (Oktober 1988):10, quoted in Lynn Underwood, *Spiritual Connection in Daily Life* (Conshocken, PA: Templeton Foundation Press, 2013), 164.

7. "Great Minds: People Who Think Good," *The Daily Show*, accessed March 16, 2015, https://www.youtube.com/watch?v=T8y5EXFMD4s.

8. "A Brief History of the Multiverse," *The New York Times*, April 12, 2003, accessed March 16, 2015,http://www.nytimes.com/2003/04/12/opinion/a-brief-history-of-the -multiverse.html accessed 3-16-2015.

9. Richard Dawkins, *The Blind Watchmaker* (New York: W. W. Norton, 1986), 46.

10. This is a common definition, as shown by "Understanding Evolution," a collaborative project of the University of California Museum of Paleontology and the National Center for Science Education, accessed June 4, 2015, http://evolution.berkeley.edu /evolibrary/article/evo_02. Darwin used the phrase "descent with modification" in his *Origin of Species*.

11. "Online Variorum of Darwin's *Origin of Species*," accessed June 4, 2015, http://darwin -online.org.uk/Variorum/1859/1859-484-c-1860.html.

12. Carl C. Gaither and Alma E. Cavazos-Gaither, *Gaither's Dictionary of Scientific Quotations* (New York: Springer Science & Business Media, 2012), 2180.

4. How Can I Believe in a God I Can't Prove?

1. C. S. Lewis, *That Hideous Strength* (1945; New York: Scribner, 1996), 190, accessed June 11, 2015, https://books.google.com/books?id=IbVTcgOyCRoC&dq =that+hideous+strength&source=gbs_navlinks_s.

2. *The Colbert Report*, accessed March 16, 2015, http://thecolbertreport.cc.com/videos/ e6ik9l/lawrence-krauss (originally aired 6/21/2012).

3. The Nicene Creed, *The United Methodist Hymnal* (Nashville: The United Methodist Publishing House, 1989), #880.

4. David Bentley Hart, *The Experience of God* (New Haven, CT: Yale University Press, 2013), 4.

5. C. S. Lewis, *Mere Christianity* (Grand Rapids: Zondervan, 1952), 38–39.

6. Charles Hartshorne, *Insights and Oversights of Great Thinkers: An Evaluation of Western Philosophy* (Albany: State University of New York Press, 1983), 101.

7. Ibid.

5. Can I Trust the Old Testament?
 1. Richard Dawkins, *The God Delusion* (New York: Houghton Mifflin Harcourt, 2008), 51.

7. Was Jesus' Resurrection Real?
 1. Daniel Defoe, *The History of the Devil* (1727), http://www.gutenberg.org/files /31053/31053-h/31053-h.htm.

2. C. S. Lewis, "Christian Apologetics," in *God in the Dock* (Grand Rapids: W. M. Eerdmans, 2014), 102.

3. Christopher Hitchens, *God Is Not Great: How Religion Poisons Everything* (New York: Hachette, 2007), 13.

4. Julian the Apostate, Letters (1923), accessed June 11, 2015, http://www.tertullian.org /fathers/julian_apostate_letters_1_trans.htm.

5. "Pope Francis: Caring for the Poor Does Not Make You a Communist," *The Independent*, October 30, 2014, accessed June 11, 2014, http://www.independent .co.uk/news/world /europe/pope-francis-caring-for-the-poor-does-not-make-you-a-communist-9828856. html.

6. *The Life of Flavius Josephus*, 75 (421), accessed June 11, 2015, http://www.ccel.org/j /josephus/works/autobiog.htm.

7. Sir Arthur Conan Doyle, *Sign of the Four,* in *The Complete Sherlock Holmes* (New York: Doubleday Bantam, 1986), 111.

8. Hart, *Atheist Delusions*, 11.

8. Why Do Christians Disagree About So Many Things?
 1. The Nicene Creed, *The United Methodist Hymnal* (Nashville: United Methodist Publishing House, 1989), #880.

2. Pew Research Center's "Global Christianity-A Report on the Size and Distribution of the World's Christian Population, http://www.pewforum.org/files/2011/12 /ChristianityAppendixB.pdf.

3. John Wesley, "Catholic Spirit," *The Works of John Wesley*, ed. Albert C. Outler (Nashville: Abingdon Press, 1985), 2:81–95.

4. John Wesley, "On the Death of George Whitfield," *The Works of John Wesley*, ed. Albert C. Outler (Nashville: Abingdon Press, 1985), 2:330–347.